SOCIAL MEDIA MARKETING FOR BEGINNERS:

SOCIAL MEDIA MARKETING FOR BEGINNERS: A STEP-BY-STEP BEGINNERS GUIDE TO FACEBOOK, INSTAGRAM, LINKEDIN MARKETING - DISCOVER NEW ONLINE TRENDS TO

SHAPE THE PERFECT STRATEGY FOR MANAGING YOUR BUSINESS.

Description

Introduction

Chapter 1 The Fundamentals of Social Media Marketing

Chapter 2 Why my business needs social media?

Chapter 3 Defining your audience

Chapter 4 Using social media platforms for marketing

Chapter 5 Social media strategy

Chapter 6 The Personal Reality of Personal Branding

Chapter 7 Don't be too professional

Chapter 8 Facebook Marketing

Chapter 9 Instagram Marketing

Chapter 10 YouTube Marketing

Chapter 11 Snapchat Marketing

Chapter 12 LinkedIn

Chapter 13 Social Media Marketing Mistakes to Avoid

Conclusion

Description

The whole world looks to be caught during a compulsive social media craze. Everyone is talking concerning using social media platforms for participating their audience, increasing believability, and building solid brands. There's a marked shift from selling to building relationships, which the social media sites do remarkably well. By definition, social media marketing is nothing however a technique of gaining traffic or audience attention for your business through the utilization of social media. The strategy usually involves concentrating marketing efforts on creating highly engaging content that attracts the attention of your target audience, and encourages them to share it throughout their virtual networks.

Unlike traditional marketing channels, social media marketing doesn't focus on hard selling (though there can be exceptions based on the nature of your business). It is about leveraging the power of audience relationships and forging strong connections through engagement. Social media marketing is concerning constantly growing your audience base by making perceptive and compelling content. It helps marketers build dramatic brands, fosters client loyalty, and lays the inspiration for marketing.

Think of your social media selling as exciting toppings on the dish of your selling combine. They add a lot of punch and panache to your selling efforts. Social media marketing makes your marketing techniques a lot of fascinating, creative, and appealing to your target audience. It adds aa lot of personal character to your robotic selling efforts.

Let's take a real-life example to establish how social media marketing works. You walk into a department store to buy lipstick or perfume. The salesperson at the counter quickly tries to understand what you want and launches into a tiresome and monotonous script about how XYZ is the bestselling fragrance or lipstick currently. You get frustrated with the whole thing because they are showing you everything that you don't want. The salesperson is not actually helping you buy, but rather trying to sell what they think you should buy. They haven't listened to you or tried to tune in to your requirements. Finally, you move to another store.

This guide will focus on the following:

- The Fundamentals of Social Media Marketing
- Why my business needs social media?
- Defining your audience
- Using social media platforms for marketing
- Social media strategy
- The Personal Reality of Personal Branding
- Be professional
- Facebook Marketing
- Instagram Marketing
- YouTube Marketing

- LinkedIn
- Snapchat Marketing
- Success Tips
- Mistakes to Avoid... AND MORE!!!

Dive in, and enjoy the process!

Introduction

Social media has traversed far greater heights than simply being a medium for user-generated content. Today, it's a tool for consumer empowerment (we all witness big conglomerates being brought to their knees by that one dissatisfied tweet or widely shared post) and a gratifying brand-consumer partnership.

Even companies that have long been dismissing social media as frivolous and flippant have started taking note of its benefits. They've realized that social media is not limited to games and light-hearted opinion polls (which are also hugely successful in creating affable brands), but can involve more serious discussions and insights that are invaluable when it comes to building strong brands.

One of the best things about social media is that it is amazingly varied and versatile. Some platforms like Pinterest and Instagram are invaluable tools for visually inclined businesses like home décor, cooking, and graphic artists. Meanwhile, channels like LinkedIn and Google+ are ideal for corporate buzz sharing. Twitter and Facebook are flexible enough to be used by businesses of almost all types. With some ingenuity and resourcefulness, even small businesses can create a storm over social media.

Unlike traditional marketing mediums, social media doesn't swallow a huge chunk of your advertising and promotion budget. You don't need to create cost-intensive and ineffectual marketing plans that leave you broke.

All you need is some creativity, perceptiveness, and an intuitive understanding about your audience's needs. More than sharp business acumen, you need a human touch. Social media gives your brand a human angle without breaking the bank.

Have you seen any of the Whole Foods videos posted on their corporate Facebook page? They frequently post how-to videos in a subject that their customers are primarily interested in – cooking. The short videos, running for about 40-60 seconds, cover multiple elements such as animation, images, and text. At the end of the video, there is an item for sale that customers can buy to prepare the recipe mentioned in the video.

One such inventive video demonstrated how customers could transform leftover Thanksgiving turkey into—hold your breath—nachos. What a refreshing change from the same old boring sandwiches! It isn't surprising that these videos are hugely popular and the products mentioned at the end are quickly grabbed up by eager viewers. They must be doing something right!

Rather than using long-winded sales pitches to glorify their products, Whole Foods is adding value to their followers' lives by sharing insanely creative ideas and making life more convenient for them. The company is showing customers ways through which their products can actually benefit them. Ingenious? Yes. Simple? Doubly yes.

Though it seems overwhelmingly complex for a beginner, especially given all the information available over the Internet, social media marketing can be relatively simple and effective.

You really do not have to be a marketing expert to master social media. All you need is some inventiveness, unwavering enthusiasm to keep learning new trends, and an empathetic touch to understand your audience.

Chapter 1 The Fundamentals of Social Media Marketing

This book will be covering methods of optimizing four platforms: Facebook, YouTube, Instagram and Pinterest. Each platform will receive its own section, where we will cover all of the tips and tricks to make the most out of each one. However, before we get to the specifics, there are quite a few fundamentals of Social Media Marketing that should be learned and understood before moving into specialization.

This section is dedicated to helping you, the reader, learn how to properly utilize Social Media for the purpose of marketing in all ways. These principles are universal, meaning that regardless of the platform that you use, they are still applicable.

Fundamental One: The Relationship Dynamic

The core of social media marketing is forming relationships with others. Social media itself is a tremendous tool for connection, an innovation that allows for unparalleled access to each other's lives. People engage with social media for a wide variety of reasons, but all of those reasons can be boiled down to one concept: they are looking for connection.

Social media allows us to connect in ways that were unthinkable in previous centuries. The ability to share information at the speed of a button click, the ability to send messages to friends halfway across the world, all of these things are meant to bring people closer together. And for the most part, social media has been wildly successful in connecting us to one another.

When people get on social media, they are looking for different experiences. Some are looking for interesting and engaging content, others are looking for things that make them laugh, but at the core, everyone is searching for something that connects to them on a deeper level. Even if they can't quite verbalize it, the truth is that people use social media as a means to find something greater than themselves.

It can be easy to approach social media marketing with a callous, removed thought process. Rather than looking at these platforms as ways of connection, we can often make the mistake of looking at them as ways of simply making money. This transactionary approach to social media isn't only ineffective, it's also extremely limiting to your potential as a business. Why? Because if we only look at social media as a means to generate revenue, we are denying the opportunity to form relationships with our customers.

Remember, people use social media because they are looking for some kind of connection. They are looking to form relationships. This might not be readily apparent from the outside, but the fact is that the most basic human need is a need to belong, the need to feel as if they are a part of something.

As a social media marketer, you don't just want sales. Sales are wonderful and vital to your business, but they aren't the only goal. Rather, the end goal of social media marketing is to create strong enough relationships with your customers that they become followers of your company and your brand. In other words, they become members of your tribe.

A tribe member isn't simply a customer, but rather they become an advocate of your product or business. They speak on your behalf. They share your content. When others ask for recommendations, they are quick to share a link to your website. They become ardent followers of your company and continue to buy your products with each release.

No doubt, a tribe member is significantly more important than a simple sale. A sale is a transaction, a tribe member is for life. The question is, how can we get people to follow our tribe? And the answer to that question is, of course, social media.

Social media allows for us to form relationships with our customers in ways that were unheard of even 15 years ago. We can answer questions directly; we can share sneak previews to those who follow our groups and we can show the heart and pulse of our brand in ways that catch the interest and attention of our followers. More importantly, we can listen to what our followers have to say. We can take heed to their words, engage in a dialogue and work with them to create a better future for our company.

For social media marketing efforts to be truly successful, it is necessary to walk the line between advertising and engaging. Of course, you want to advertise your products, get them to visit your links and generate sales, but you cannot neglect the social aspect. If you work on forming relationships first, the sales will come rolling in. However, if you neglect building relationships with your customers and only focus on promoting your products, you may get sales, but you certainly won't get tribe members.

So how can we form these relationships? How can we create these bonds that turn a customer into a follower? Let's look at the second fundamental to learn more.

Fundamental Two: Focus on Customers First by Creating Value

When an individual is browsing through social media, they are searching for things that provide them some sort of benefit. We would refer to this benefit simply as value. They are searching for valuable things to them. Different customers find different ideas valuable. For example, a serious businessman would find a blog article about improving office workflow to be of great value. A teenager would find a funny meme to be just as valuable to himself.

Value is what drives engagement. Followers do not engage with content that doesn't provide value to their lives. In other words, unless they are getting something out of the exchange, they won't care. There are a million other things on the internet that they could be looking at, so if it doesn't appeal to them in some way, they will ignore it.

Effective social media marketing requires that we develop a keen understanding of how to create and provide value to our followers. The reason for this is twofold:

1. If a customer finds your content to be valuable, they will follow you.
2. By providing them with something they need, you are signaling that you care about them.

Ineffective social media marketing tends to be highly self-focused. The assumption is that all one needs to do is post a few dozen times a week, all talking about your product or business and the job is done. However, this type of posting strategy doesn't work nearly as well as one would hope. Mainly because people are not interested in what you have to say about yourself, at least until they are interested in you. And the only way to get them interested in you is to provide them with some kind of incentive to pay attention.

Conversational narcissism must be avoided when it comes to social media marketing. It's all well and fine to make a post here and there about your company or products, but if those are the only types of content that you release, people will not take you too seriously.

Instead, you should work to identify what your consumer base values are. After that, you should work to aggregate and create content that reflect these values. Blog posts, articles, pictures and infographics are all excellent types of content that draw the viewer in and gets them to engage with you.

The more that you focus on your customers' needs and wants, the better chances you have of capturing their attention. And once you have their attention, you will be able to then show them your own products or services. In other words, to get what you want, you have to give them what they want. This is the give and take nature of social media. Everyone on Facebook or Instagram is looking for content that provides value to their lives.

Fundamental Three: Organic Marketing Has a Limit

Organic marketing is the process of marketing through the natural methods of using a social media platform. Making a post that is shown to 300 followers is organic marketing. It happens naturally and costs you nothing. When first getting started, organic marketing has quite the allure to it. The ability to gain customers without paying a dime sounds too good to be true. And in some ways, it is possible for you to generate customers and sales through organic marketing. The simple act of having a Facebook or Instagram page can bring in potential sales, especially if people are sharing your posts with their friends.

However, there are limits to your ability to market organically. The biggest limit is that all social media companies themselves, Facebook, Twitter, Instagram, are all interested in selling advertising space to companies. That is how these companies make money, they generate large user bases and then sell advertisers ad space to reach that user base.

This means that social media platforms have strong incentive to push business accounts towards paying for advertisements. They incentivize this behavior by limiting the amount that an organic, unpaid post can reach. For example, Facebook will limit your ability to reach followers when you post. You may have 1,000 followers, but your post will only show up in about 200 feeds. This is because Facebook doesn't want you using their services for free. They would rather that you pay a fee and promote your post instead, reaching all of your followers.

Ultimately, organic marketing has limitations. You can work for a while, growing your brand, increasing your following and generating sales through unpaid, organic marketing, but it won't nearly be as efficient as paid marketing. On top of that, organic marketing is slower and doesn't yield the same level of results that a highly targeted ad campaign would be. This isn't to say that there is no place for organic marketing, just that you shouldn't expect to be able to seriously market on social media without investing money in ads.

Fundamental Four: Social Media is a Means to an End, Not the End Itself

It can be easy to get caught up in focusing entirely on social media, especially since your task is to market through it. It's easy to get sucked into the idea of wanting to grow your social media pages as much as possible. Getting a lot of likes and page follows can be addicting, and if you're not careful, you could potentially lose sight of the purpose of social media marketing. Social media marketing isn't about increasing your popularity or growing your page, rather it is about helping customers move through a sales funnel, to the end step of making a conversion.

This means your main focus shouldn't be on simply increasing your popularity on any given platform, rather you should be focusing on developing a system of moving people through each step of the funnel. Social media platforms are incredible tools for creating awareness, excitement and desire for a product, but the goal is to eventually move your follower off of social media and onto a platform where you have full control.

Social media is inherently competitive when it comes to attention. A follower may be looking at your post one minute, but the next they may get a message or see another post and become distracted. You only have half of the customer's attention for as long as they are on the social media platform. On top of that, you also have to work with the confines and limitations that these platforms have. You don't have full control, which limits your ability to properly market your products and services.

Instead of looking at social media as the end goal, you should look at it as a means of capturing interest and generating awareness. Then, once that awareness and interest has been captured, social media can move these potential customers to your domain, where you will better be able to advertise to them.

To summarize, the fundamentals of social media marketing is creating relationships, providing followers with valuable content, realizing organic marketing has inherent limitations and that the ultimate end goal is to move customers to your own domains. These are the four basic building blocks to any successful social media marketing campaign. Whether you're using Facebook, Instagram or any other social media platform, these principles apply.

CREATE VALUABLE CONTENT

Social media is powered by sharing content. They are looking for some kind of content that adds something to their lives. One of your primary jobs as a social media marketer is to create or aggregate valuable content, so that they can be shared through your chosen social media outlets.

This isn't a simple or easy task, but it is necessary. Content is king, as the old adage goes. As long as you are able to generate unique and valuable content for users, you will be able to capture interest, create leads and gain a following. Ultimately, you will be able to convert those followers into tribe members, especially if your content is good enough to keep them coming back for more and more.

Understanding Content Types:

At the core, content is meant to provide a solution to a customer's problem. In basic terms, the problem is that the customer needs something and the solution is the content you are providing. For example, a common problem is that a customer is bored. You solve that problem by providing content that entertains them. This is the primary way that you will foster connection with customers. Provide good content, gain a follower.

There are several different types of content, geared towards solving different problems. We can break them down into three basic categories: Entertainment, Information and Assistance.

Entertainment:

Entertainment is one of the most universal types of content that exists online. People are always looking for some kind of distraction from their problems and the real world. Entertainment often solves this problem by providing interesting and enjoyable experiences that make them smile, make them think or make them laugh. Entertainment content can be as simple as a picture of a cat with captions, or as complex as a long YouTube video.

Information:

Education is another extremely popular form of content. The internet has enabled people to learn just about anything out there and millions of people each day are scouring the internet, looking for information about their particular interests or niches. Providing high quality education and information content is a surefire way of developing a steady following.

Assistance:

Assistance is a type of content that is an offshoot of information. Rather than simply just providing information or education, assistance is where you generate content that actively works to solve their problem. This could be a how-to video, a step by step instructional blog post or a visual guide. Assistance content is extremely valuable because it shows that you care enough about your customers to provide them with free ways of solving their own problems.

Collecting Content:

There are two different ways that you can acquire content to be shared through social media. The first is to aggregate content, which means that you go online, find a bunch of pre-existing content that does not belong to you and then share it on your page.

Content aggregation is a perfectly fine strategy, provided that you give proper credit to the individuals who actually created the content. You can scour the internet, collect great content and share it with others, all without having to go through the process of creating the content yourself. This is a great way to fill the bulk of your posts with good, relevant content.

There are some downsides to content aggregation. The biggest is that this content won't play into your brand or direct people toward your websites. Rather, these pieces of content will exist simply as a means of generating interest in your profile. You may gain followers out of the deal, but you won't have the opportunity to direct them to your website.

The second type of content is original content, created and produced by you. Original content is extremely valuable, especially in social media platforms, where people often come across the same, unoriginal content over and over again.

Original content allows for you to present your company brand and direct people to your website through the inclusion of watermarks or even direct links to your domains. If people like your content and begin to share it, there is a chance that your content could bring in a wider array of viewers. This could potentially translate to an increased following or even conversions!

The downside to original content creation is that you have to spend time, effort and in some cases, money to be able to create that content. Content comes in all different shapes and sizes, but at the end of the day, it has to be created by hand. Let's take a look at the most popular types of content that can be created.

Blog Posts:

Long form written content remains to be one of the most popular types of content out there. People love to read articles. By utilizing a blog, you can generate blog posts that can then be dispersed through social media. This will achieve two major goals: creating awareness of your business and directing them to your website. Of course, they won't be visiting your website for any other reason than to see your blog, but you have a chance of converting them to at least following your blog for updates periodically. And once they have finished reading the post that interested them, they might poke around some more on your site, which could increase your chances of an organic sale.

Infographics:

Infographics are exceptionally popular because they combine strong visuals with information. People often enjoy reading infographics and are quick to share them, especially if they find them to be well made. Creating infographics does require both visual design skill as well as properly documented sources, which requires research time.

Pictures:

Memes, drawings, illustrations or simple photographs tend to be shared the most due to their simplicity. People can quickly glance at the content, get an understanding of it and then experience wonder, humor or excitement. While pictures most likely won't direct them to your website directly, they are still great ways to entertain your followers and provide them with the content that they care about.

Video:

Videos are another type of popular content that people like to engage with and share. We'll be covering this subject more in depth in the YouTube section, which is the primary outlet for not only creating videos, but also for sharing them through multiple social media platforms.

These four types of content make up what most social media users enjoy interacting with on a daily basis. As a social media marketer, you're going to want to have an established schedule of creating, collecting and releasing these types of content on your chosen platforms. The more content that you are able to release, the more your followers will engage.

It's important to remember that the content you're distributing isn't meant to promote or actively sell your products. Those types of posts aren't considered to be content, rather they are considered to be advertisements. While it's perfectly fine to sprinkle in an ad here or there in your posting schedule, you're going to want to focus primarily on releasing content that is for the benefit of your followers. This will help generate goodwill, increase their interest in your profile page and gain you followers.

Over time, the more people who engage with your content will become more receptive to the ads that you do end up posting. After all, you have proven to them that you genuinely do care about them by giving them the things that they want. This back and forth, give and take relationship are the backbone of a successful social media marketing strategy.

Chapter 2 Why my business needs social media?

At this point, not being present on social media is like flipping through a telephone book to find the number of your hairdresser. Or still owning a Nokia 3310. And while there is nothing wrong with using a two-decade-old cell phone model or keeping it old-school with hand-written telephone books, one thing is certain – those people miss out on the perks of today's technology. And that's perfectly fine. If you are just a guy who has a no-modern-technology principle, that is. But if you are a business that is looking for a way to increase the conversion and reap as many benefits as possible, then being present online is a must.

For many people social media is the internet, so they spend their hours scrolling down their social media platforms. Why? Because there is no reason to leave, actually. From chatting with people, to being up-to-date with news and finding and buying products and services, the social networks literally have it all. If you want your business to be successful, then having a strong social media presence is of great essence.

If your business is still not active on social media, then that is definitely the missing link that can strengthen the connection between your product/service and your customers. Still not sure whether it is worth the time and effort? Here are the benefits of being present on the social networks:

Web Traffic

Marketing your business on social media is a crucial part for your web traffic:

Posting on Social Media Drives Your Targeted Audience

Of course you want your business to be the first thing people will see when surfing the internet for similar products/services. But is that really possible if you are not active online? Posting regularly on social media will help you take domination over the first search page which will, in turn, increase your profits.

These social media posts are extremely valuable for increasing web traffic. For instance, think about what happens when you update your website. It surely takes a while for it to get traction with the search engines, right? That means that the number of customers that will be aware of your new content will be limited. Posting on social media will help your potential customers find your new content easily and then be re-directed to your website. This means that you don't have to wait for a customer to click on your website to find out your updates. Social media allows you to reach potential customers even if they are not looking to buy at that exact moment,

Social Media Posts Boosts the SEO

Search engine optimization is of great importance for your online presence and overall business. Don't be fooled that this is not that important. SEO experts know which sites have constant traffic and which sits lonely and forgotten. A great content strategy can obviously skyrocket your search rankings, however, social media posts also have the power to drive more traffic to your site. By re-sharing popular content you can easily optimize your page and lure existing and potential customers to take a peek. The boosted traffic will then lead to inbound clicks and will have a significant impact on your prominence in Google rankings.

Quoting Can Make You More Reachable

Sometimes, a simple quote can throw more traffic your way. Whether you have used a PR tool such as HARO to find experts for your site or you simply want to quote an expert with a strong influence on social media, this can surely help your business. Chances are, by quoting (and tagging!) an expert in your tweet or Facebook post, that person will most likely share or retweet your post which will help you reach potential customers from their list of followers and increase your site's traffic.

Connecting with Customers

Being the bridge that can connect the gap between you and your customers, social media is definitely the shortcut you need to take in order to reach your audience the fastest way possible.

Reaching Customers

Social media is perhaps the only tool that can help you reach customers from all age groups at once. These networks are not just for teenagers searching for entertainment. The social media platforms are actively used by more than 2.7 billion people, so it is safe to say that whatever your target audience is, your potential customers are spending some efficient time on social media already. In fact, a study has actually found that 37% of all the Americans over 65 years of age are social media users.

Whether you want to reach young adults, housewives, or retirees, social media is the best place to introduce your product/service to them.

Besides, advertising on social media allows targeting and retargeting your audience which can play a crucial role in your marketing strategy. For instance, the ads on Facebook can be filtered around the needs of your customers and target only the age, location, industry, etc. of the audience that you are trying to reach.

Learning about Your Target Audience

Perhaps the biggest reason why social media marketing is so game-changing for businesses is the fact that these networks actually allow you to have a real interaction with your existing and potential customers. This creates an incredible opportunity to peek inside your audience's lives and learn about the customer behaviors first-hand. By reading posts and tweets, you can easily find the answers to the questions that every business is mostly concerned with:

- *What product/services do people want to buy and why?*
- *What kind of websites do people mostly visit?*
- *What are the biggest hobbies nowadays and how can my product/service help?*
- *What types of posts do people share the most?*

Finding the answers to these questions will help you understand your customers and allow you to write compelling posts and tweets that people will find appealing. By retweeting and sharing, you will not only increase the traffic and eventually profits, but also pinpoint what are the disappointments of the customers and how to refine your product/service in order to increase conversion.

Getting Noticed Easily

Imagine that you are hosting an event. A decent promotion is kind of required, right? What best way to do it than to have an active social media presence? Social media platforms will help you spread the word which will not only bring more guests, but can also throw a few big perks your way such as finding donors that are eager to participate.

Improving Your Brand's Image

Marketing your product/service on social media can help you thrive as a company, increase the exposure of your brand, and make its image recognizable and trustworthy.

The Best Customer Service Tool

Building a great image for your brand starts with keeping your customers happy and content. Many studies have shown that customers mostly reward those companies that take the time to quickly respond to their inquiries. But quickly responding to complaints isn't what it used to be. If there is a customer request pending, they are expecting for the issue to be solved right away.

Social media helps you offer customer service that is quick, helpful, and proactive, and gives you the opportunity to reach and help your customers before they get the chance to call your call center. This little trick just saved British Telecom over 2 million pounds in customer service costs, so just let that sink in for a second.

Building Up the Loyalty of Your Brand

This is actually pretty self-explanatory, but it would be remiss not to mention it. By taking the time to engage with your customers actively and provide them with beneficial info, help with inquiries, and keep them entertained without asking a thing in return, your brand's loyalty is actually enhanced.

The right social media presence can bring value to the customers and show them that you are not looking to empty their pockets, but that you actually care whether they are satisfied with your product/service or not.

Chapter 3 Defining your audience

As we discussed earlier, defining your audience is essential to creating your own personal brand. It is the process of examining your body of work and what you have to offer, followed by an intense dive into market research and what it tells you about how well or poorly you and your content will sell among different demographics. Defining your audience also entails conducting your own personal research as well as introducing common sense into the equation. You do not have to pay a market research analyst money to figure out that your fashion blog geared towards LGBTQIA youth is not going to circulate well in the over 65 communities of Boca Raton, Florida. While every person is an individual and it can seem cold or even heartless and sociopathic to boil people down to demographics and age ranges and taste, but at the end of the day it is not going to be worth your limited time and resources to market to an entire community for the sake of reaching your snowflake consumer.

Defining your audience is also essential because as you may already know, once you have a defined your group of interest and best possible marketing opportunities, you can now begin to target that audience with your branding. This can mean running ads in media that you know members of your key demographic are likely to tune in to, as well as deciding to research the ways in which you can better serve the people who will hopefully become your financial supporters. Let us say, for example, that you are targeting men and women in their 30's and 40's who are interested in cooking. You create a cooking channel on YouTube and write a weekly blog about all things happening in the kitchen. Since you know who will be most likely to tune into your channel, read your blogs, and follow you on social media, you should consider what kinds of things people in this age range and demographic enjoy most. Your recipes are made from simple ingredients and sometimes premade things, so you know that your target audience is most likely people who work and do not have a great deal of time or money to spend on every meal, but still want to make them taste good and be nutritious. You could write several posts periodically about the importance of balancing time with quality preparation in the kitchen. You could make sure to use less professional techniques and make your videos easy to follow and recreate at home. You could partner with brands that are available in the lesser-expensive grocery stores when sponsoring products or having videos paid for.

Ultimately, defining your audience will help you to conduct a better, more targeted effort in your personal brand, and it simply involves identifying your audience, then getting to know them and the things that they value, then implementing that into your branding technique. You can even cater to your audience without compromising yourself in professional branding. Yes, it is somewhat more difficult to know what a potential employer wants as they do not publish market research reports on such things, but you can deduce what type of things they are looking for simply by getting to know more about the company. Read their website and memorize their company values. If you have the time, prior to an interview or submitting a resume, include some of those keywords into your social media posts. See what kinds of coworkers they have hired. Are there any common traits you see? Get to know what your potential employer wants to see and hear from an ideal candidate, and do your best to implement that into your own brand and delivery. Defining your audience is simply identifying who is most likely to buy what you are branding, and then giving them what they would like most. Learn to empathize with your audience and make them feel comfortable when taking in everything you have to offer.

Chapter 4 Using social media platforms for marketing

Dominating social media in actuality is going to require you to focus your social media platform with a clear approach, defined goals, and a strategy that will help you reach those goals. Creating a multi-platform approach requires you to know how to leverage each platform, how you can build a massive following on each platform, and then how to turn that platform into a working social media sales funnel. Before you can start creating your strategy and determining how to grow on each platform, you need to decide what your goals are and how you can best reach those goals using social media. Each platform is going to provide you with slightly different benefits. So, by identifying your goals first, you can ensure that you are going to be using the right platforms and enforcing the right strategies to maximize your time investment on social media.

Creating Your Business Goals

The first thing you want to do is create your business goals for these year. Typically, all of your other strategic goals should directly reflect your overall business goals. By knowing exactly what it is that you are trying to accomplish in your business in the immediate future, you can start creating goals for your social media platforms as well. You can set one or more goals for your business in the near future, though you should be intentional about setting only one or two goals as your primary focus for the year. This way, you are clear on exactly what it is that you are working toward and you can design every secondary goal and strategy around that primary goal in your business.

The best way to create your business goal is to look at what means the most to you and your business for the coming year and create your goals around that concept. If you are brand new in business, you might set the goal to make your first year profitable in business. Identify what exact number that would be for you. Or, you might set the goal to increase your brand awareness and start connecting with a broader audience so that you have a system of trusted people to invest in your business as you continue to grow your brand name and popularity over the years to come. If you have been in business longer, your goal may be to refocus your brand on something slightly different and bring your audience along on that adjustment with you. You might try to increase your profits this year so that you can hire more employees or offer more to your audience.

Whatever your goals may be, make sure that you use the S.M.A.R.T planning goal style to ensure that you are setting goals that you can actually achieve this same year. So, your goals need to be specific, measurable, attainable, realistic, and timely. For example, rather than saying "I want to earn a six-figure year in these year " you could say "I want to earn

$125,000 in revenue by December 31, of these year through my business." When you set specific goals, it becomes easier for you to know whether or not you are effectively moving toward your goals. This way you can determine if your strategies are working or if they need to be adjusted to help you advance more effectively.

Creating Your Social Media Goals

Once you have your general business goals created, you can start determining what your social media goals are going to be. It is important to realize that social media works differently for different business models. Approaching your social media goals requires you to consider what exactly social media can do for you and how you can maintain your image while incorporating social media into your strategy. For example, if you are a lawyer, you may not want to use social media as openly as another business because you cannot freely share certain information. In certain industries, you will need to be more conservative in your approach, which means that your goals should reflect these conservative social media values. So, if you were a lawyer on Instagram, rather than being open and sharing snippets of your life online, you would likely refrain from using stories or IGTV altogether and instead simply create posts on your feed. These posts should be targeted specifically toward your desired audience by providing them with the information that they need to know, then direct them to your website or your phone number so that you can talk privately with them. In this scenario, your social media goals would be to entirely get people to contact you, rather than to build a massive following and become a well-liked influencer in your industry.

You can determine which style of social media goals you need quite simply. If you run a more professional business where you need to keep a large portion of information private, then you need to use social media to drive people to contact you. If you run a brick and mortar store, then you need to use social media to drive people into your store so that they can shop with you. If you run an online business, then you need to build your following so that you can market to a larger audience.

That being said, you still need to be more specific when you are setting social media goals. What *exactly* are you trying to achieve through social media? For example, if you are the owner of a coffee shop, do you want to drive more tourists to your coffee shop so that they can take pictures with your photo ops and increase the popularity of your shop? Or, do you want to increase the amount of local individuals who are coming through your doors to purchase coffee and become loyal visitors? If you are an influencer, maybe you want to increase your following so that you can generate pitches for popular brands and start earning more income through your platform.

Whatever it is that you desire to do, make sure that you are utilizing social media as a tool in your overall goals and not relying on it as the exclusive strategy itself. Even if social media is your primary method for reaching out to your audience, you should recognize that your business itself is not exclusive to social media. You will still have plenty of other things that need to happen in order for you to achieve your goals. When you see social media as a tool and organize it into your overall strategy as a tool, you put yourself in the position where you can start using social media as one of your most powerful forces online.

Determining What Platforms Will Work Best for You

After determining what your goals are for social media, you have one last thing that you need to consider before beginning the process of designing your social media strategy. You need to determine what platforms are going to be the most effective for you when it comes to achieving the goals that you have set out to achieve. In each of the following sections, you are going to learn about the six biggest social media platforms that presently exist, how they can be used, and who will most benefit from them. Make sure that you read through this information and choose platforms that are actually going to support you in achieving your goals so that you are focusing your efforts in areas that make sense to your overall goals and business.

Chapter 5 Social media strategy

Creating Your Goals

Dominating social media in 2019 is going to require you to focus your social media platform with a clear approach, defined goals, and a strategy that will help you reach those goals. Creating a multi-platform approach requires you to know how to leverage each platform, how you can build a massive following on each platform, and then how to turn that platform into a working social media sales funnel. Before you can start creating your strategy and determining how to grow on each platform, you need to decide what your goals are and how you can best reach those goals using social media. Each platform is going to provide you with slightly different benefits. So, by identifying your goals first, you can ensure that you are going to be using the right platforms and enforcing the right strategies to maximize your time investment on social media.

Creating Your Business Goals

The first thing you want to do is create your business goals for 2019. Typically, all of your other strategic goals should directly reflect your overall business goals. By knowing exactly what it is that you are trying to accomplish in your business in 2019, you can start creating goals for your social media platforms as well. You can set one or more goals for your business in 2019, though you should be intentional about setting only one or two goals as your primary focus for the year. This way, you are clear on exactly what it is that you are working toward and you can design every secondary goal and strategy around that primary goal in your business.

The best way to create your business goal is to look at what means the most to you and your business for the coming year and create your goals around that concept. If you are brand new in business, you might set the goal to make your first year profitable in business. Identify what exact number that would be for you. Or, you might set the goal to increase your brand awareness and start connecting with a broader audience so that you have a system of trusted people to invest in your business as you continue to grow your brand name and popularity over the years to come. If you have been in business longer, your goal may be to refocus your brand on something slightly different and bring your audience along on that adjustment with you. You might try to increase your profits this year so that you can hire more employees or offer more to your audience.

Whatever your goals may be, make sure that you use the S.M.A.R.T planning goal style to ensure that you are setting goals that you can actually achieve in 2019. So, your goals need to be specific, measurable, attainable, realistic, and timely. For example, rather than saying "I want to earn a six-figure year in 2019" you could say "I want to earn $125,000 in revenue by

December 31, 2019 through my business." When you set specific goals, it becomes easier for you to know whether or not you are effectively moving toward your goals. This way you can determine if your strategies are working or if they need to be adjusted to help you advance more effectively.

Creating Your Social Media Goals

Once you have your general business goals created, you can start determining what your social media goals are going to be. It is important to realize that social media works differently for different business models. Approaching your social media goals requires you to consider what exactly social media can do for you and how you can maintain your image while incorporating social media into your strategy. For example, if you are a lawyer, you may not want to use social media as openly as another business because you cannot freely share certain information. In certain industries, you will need to be more conservative in your approach, which means that your goals should reflect these conservative social media values. So, if you were a lawyer on Instagram, rather than being open and sharing snippets of your life online, you would likely refrain from using stories or IGTV altogether and instead simply create posts on your feed. These posts should be targeted specifically toward your desired audience by providing them with the information that they need to know, then direct them to your website or your phone number so that you can talk privately with them. In this scenario, your social media goals would be to entirely get people to contact you, rather than to build a massive following and become a well-liked influencer in your industry.

You can determine which style of social media goals you need quite simply. If you run a more professional business where you need to keep a large portion of information private, then you need to use social media to drive people to contact you. If you run a brick and mortar store, then you need to use social media to drive people into your store so that they can shop with you. If you run an online business, then you need to build your following so that you can market to a larger audience.

That being said, you still need to be more specific when you are setting social media goals. What *exactly* are you trying to achieve through social media? For example, if you are the owner of a coffee shop, do you want to drive more tourists to your coffee shop so that they can take pictures with your photo ops and increase the popularity of your shop? Or, do you want to increase the amount of local individuals who are coming through your doors to purchase coffee and become loyal visitors? If you are an influencer, maybe you want to increase your following so that you can generate pitches for popular brands and start earning more income through your platform.

Whatever it is that you desire to do, make sure that you are utilizing social media as a tool in your overall goals and not relying on it as the exclusive strategy itself. Even if social media is your primary method for reaching out to your audience, you should recognize that your business itself is not exclusive to social media. You will still have plenty of other things that need to happen in order for you to achieve your goals. When you see social media as a tool and organize it into your overall strategy as a tool, you put yourself in the position where you can start using social media as one of your most powerful forces online.

Determining What Platforms Will Work Best for You

After determining what your goals are for social media, you have one last thing that you need to consider before beginning the process of designing your social media strategy. You need to determine what platforms are going to be the most effective for you when it comes to achieving the goals that you have set out to achieve. In each of the following sections, you are going to learn about the six biggest social media platforms that presently exist, how they can be used, and who will most benefit from them. Make sure that you read through this information and choose platforms that are actually going to support you in achieving your goals so that you are focusing your efforts in areas that make sense to your overall goals and business.

Harmful Risks "Experts" Tell You

With the rise of the social media empire, unfortunately, there are many "experts" out there who are sharing harmful myths about social media marketing and how people can utilize social media platforms to build a strong presence for their brand. These "experts" tend to be quite persuasive, which can lead to many individuals following them only to find themselves being fed bad information that stops them from being able to grow the online presence that they desire.

Before you get started creating your official strategies and getting your brand online, it is important that you understand what these myths are and how they can negatively impact your business if you are not careful. Chances are, you have already heard at least one of these myths which is why it is important that you learn the truth first, to avoid having you go into the process of building your online brand while believing this information to be true.

Myth #1: Social Media Analytics Are Not Important

The first big myth that many self-proclaimed experts will tell you is that your analytics are not important. This myth comes through in two ways. One states that as long as you are getting "some" engagement on each post, you are doing well, the other states that even if you are getting no engagement, people are still seeing your posts. These myths obviously come from people who do not understand social media marketing or the purpose of social media marketing.

Analytics on social media tell you exactly what people like, what they want more of, and how you can share with them in a way that actually creates traction and success in your brand. When you look at your analytics, you can see exactly what posts people are enjoying the most, and you can emulate these posts to begin making even more success in your online platform. You *want* to be doing this because, in doing so, you can ensure that you are actually being seen by the right people. If your posts are not getting enough traction or if your engagement is not regularly growing, it is because you are missing a step or doing something wrong. As long as you are listening to what your audience likes by paying attention to the analytics, there is no reason why your online platform should not be growing on a consistent basis.

In regard to whether or not "no engagement" means that your posts are still being "seen," this is simply not how social media works. Posts that are not engaged with are hidden from timelines as social media platforms will assume that these posts are irrelevant and that they are simply cluttering up individuals' newsfeeds. People like to see posts that are relevant or interesting and since social media caters to its users, it will favor showing these posts over any other posts. That means, if you have posts that are regularly being ignored, it is likely because no one is seeing them; not because they "are seeing them but are afraid to engage for fear of being sold to" as many perceived experts will attempt to tell you.

Myth #2: Social Media Is Only for Creating New Customers
If you have ever heard that social media is specifically meant for gaining new customers, then you have heard another common myth in the social media marketing world. The truth is, social media is not exclusively for creating new customers, it is also for retaining customers. In fact, a recent study showed that 84% of most brands on Facebook are being followed by people who were customers *first* and who went on to find them on social media, not by new customers who have never shopped with the brand at all.

This statistic likely varies across all of the different platforms, but the fact remains that social media is a powerful tool for staying in touch with your existing audience and maintaining their loyalty. When you encourage your existing customers to follow you, you create the opportunity to maintain and grow your relationship with them, which supports you in bringing existing customers back and turning them into loyal fans of your brand.

In fact, when you are on social media, you should be targeting your existing audience as much as you target your new audience, since your existing audience will be the ones already prepared to share their experiences of their company with others. If you cater to them and connect with them online, this makes it easier for them to share their reviews of your brand with their friends and family, and hopefully, drive more attention to your brand and traffic to your business. For that reason, you should be targeting your existing audience often and create a platform that is just as enjoyable for them to follow as it is for new followers to find you.

Myth #3: Ignore Negative Feedback or Commentary
Receiving negative feedback or comments on your brand can be hurtful, especially if you are closely connected with your company or if you are your own brand. Hearing what other people are saying, especially when what they are saying is not nice, can feel like a deep and painful insult and it can make running your own business challenging.

Initially, you may even feel like leaving the social media world to avoid having a platform for negative feedback like this to come in, though that would not be effective in helping you reach the people you desired. If you look around on the net, a common statement made by self-proclaimed social media experts is that you should simply ignore negative commentary and feedback because engaging with "trolls" is not helpful to your business.

However, this is actually an extremely negative way to handle negative commentary and it can lead to your business and brand being viewed as ignorant or even suspicious. As well, when you ignore the negative commentary, you assume that everyone who has something bad to say is a "troll" or someone who is trying to bash your company when, in reality, it may just be someone who previously liked your company but encountered a bad experience. In other words, you could use this as an opportunity to change someone's mind about your brand and build a loyal follower if you play your cards right. Even if you can't, and the person truly is just someone who has nothing nice to say, not handling the situation effectively can make other potentially interested customers less interested in your brand.

The best way to handle negative commentary is to kindly respond back thanking the individual for leaving feedback, apologizing for their negative experience, and offering a solution to rectify it. Or, if the comment was left by someone who is not your client, you might consider responding kindly to let them know that you see and hear them, that you appreciate their concerns, and that you will rectify the situation as appropriate.

Here are three examples of different types of comments that you might experience online and ways that you can kindly and appropriately handle them. Notice that each strategy puts you on the record as being a company that listens, cares, and serves rather than one that simply ignores people and their problems.

Comment #1:

Follower: "In the past I used (company) products until, I purchased one of their new [products] and the quality was really bad! It broke within the first week. The quality of this [company] has really gone downhill since the beginning. Shame, too. They used to be so good!"

You: "Hi [follower]! We are so sorry to hear about your negative experience, that is definitely not what we want! I can assure you that quality is still a priority when it comes to the products we create. Can you please contact us at [customer care info] so we can rectify your experience?"

Comment #2:

Follower: "I heard this company is horrible, my friend tried their products and felt ripped off. I will never waste my money here!"

You: "Hi [follower]! We are so sorry to hear that your friend had a negative experience. We pride ourselves in offering high quality products to our clients. Do you know if your friend contacted our customer care team to receive support in rectifying the situation? We would love to pass this along to our quality control department to ensure that this does not happen again."

Comment #3:

Follower: "Nice try! I've seen products like this before, they're a complete waste. Don't spend your money on something like this!"

You: "Hi [follower]! We're sorry to hear that you will not be giving our products a try because you think these products are a waste. Not all companies create [this product] equally, so you might be surprised to learn that ours stands out due to its [highlight points.] We hope you'll give it a try!"

When you handle comments properly, you show existing customers that you care and that you want them to have a positive experience, and you show new customers that you are not simply trying to make money through unethical or illegitimate sales strategies. Since there are so many companies on the internet, setting yourself apart from others is imperative to let your audience know that you are a genuine company that stands in alignment with integrity and high-quality products. This way, people will be more likely to shop with you because they trust that if they have a negative experience for any reason that you will support them in rectifying that experience.

Myth #4: "Blank" Is Dead

Every single year, blog posts and other articles report that a certain platform is "dead" or is falling off the face of the map. This marketing strategy has been used for years to try and capture attention, drive people away from certain platforms, and gain followers on others. The truth is, no online platform has truly died unless no one is using it anymore.

Instead, these reports are often being shared by people who are using the wrong platforms, and therefore, are unable to connect with their desired audience. As a result, they believe said platform is dead when in reality, they are simply not utilizing the right platforms in the right ways to gain access to their audience.

If you read posts like this, take a moment to read through the active statistics of the platform that is claimed to have "died" because in most cases, these statistics will prove that the platform is not going anywhere. These are just another example of false marketing experts attempting to create traction in their business by creating clickbait content that holds no value or fact. Avoid marketers or experts who use claims like these, as they will likely lead you astray from the truth. Also, they may not be able to give you the proper guidance that you need to generate success in the online space.

Myth #5: If It's Not Selling, It's Not Marketing
At one time, most individuals who were using social media were marketing by sharing advertisement-looking posts repeatedly with an attempt to share products and services with their audiences. Since social media was so young and new at the time, these strategies worked and many people made a lot of money using these strategies. However, this strategy no

longer works. Ultimately, too many people started using it and most followers grew to feel like they were reading through magazines filled with advertisements rather than social media timelines that were intended to connect loved ones and friends over the internet.

These days, the best way to build your business online is to focus on the social aspect of social media first and then tie in your sales after. There is a rule that suggests that you share your marketing content using an 80/20 rule, where you share 80% personal content and 20% sales posts so that people can get to know you more often than they are being sold to by you. This strategy is known as "attraction marketing" and it happens to be one of the most powerful strategies in today's online marketplace.

The reason why this strategy works, especially if you are running an exclusively online business, is because you are putting your relationships with others above your sales numbers. When people see this, they start feeling connected to you and they personally care about you and the message that you are sharing with your audience. They feel a sense of trust and understanding which leads to them feeling passionate about what you do and who you are, which helps them become people who are openly willing and eager to purchase from you when you do market your products to your audience.

So, just because every single post does not end with a sales pitch does not mean that it is not marketing. It simply means that some of your posts are marketing your brand and building brand awareness, and others are actually asking for sales and inviting people to buy into your product or services. In this day and age, this strategy is far more effective and productive than any other strategy. So, do not believe anyone who tries to tell you that you must somehow twist every single post into a sales pitch. This is simply not true.

Chapter 6 The Personal Reality of Personal Branding

Before digging into the mechanisms of what it takes to develop a personal brand, first, it is a good idea to explore what a personal brand truly is so that you can decide whether or not you are ready to have one. Even if you already have a brand, if you are struggling to grow at the rate which you desire, reading this chapter will help you equip yourself with the right tools to approach your personal growth effectively. Personal branding is all the rage right now and, in one way or another, many people use it as a tool to develop their reputations and leverage their reputation to earn better opportunities in life. That being said, some people personally brand by leveraging their reputation to gain more in life, and people who brand as an intentional tool that helps them develop a profitable business. If you are reading this book, the chances are that you want to develop your very own profitable business by leveraging your brand, which is an incredible idea!

Before you get started, understanding what it takes out of you as a person to run your brand is important. Many people start their businesses with a lack of awareness regarding the development of their brand on a personal level. Of course, the way these particular brands develop is different from your average brand because they are based on you as a person, rather than a separate entity that you have developed for your brand itself. For that reason alone, there is plenty of personal work, commitment, and effort that goes into creating your brand. Ideally, you should be prepared to take on all of this personal work to allow yourself to grow into the fullest potential of your personal brand and truly make the most out of your efforts. In this chapter, you are going to explore what these things are, how they may impact you, and what you can do to ensure that you grow through them rather than find yourself feeling trapped or stuck under a difficult mountain of growth.

Keep Your Mind Open

When it comes to personal branding, you must keep an open mind if you are going to grow through all of the obstacles that you will face along the way. Personal branding may be straight forward on paper, but when it comes to applying what you have learned, you will need to discover how you can mentally stay on track to continue applying the steps day after day. For someone who has never been in branding before, it can take some time to "learn the ropes" and discover how you are going to get yourself out there and grow. For some people, developing a brand is largely about having freedom, which can lead to a lack of work ethic and an inability to stay committed, and for others, it is easy to stay focused and keep working away. If you find that you are someone who struggles to stay focused, you will need to keep your mind open to learn about new ways that you can continue applying yourself, even when it feels challenging to stay committed.

Another reason why you want to keep an open mind is that developing your brand can be challenging if you stay too attached to your original idea. You need to have a strong vision for what you want to create, while also remaining flexible in how it looks and the steps that you will take to get there. To put it simply, you do not know everything right now, and as you learn and develop your brand more, your vision will evolve over time. Keeping an open mind will allow you to continue developing your brand so that you can easily allow yourself to continue building without attempting to confine yourself to a dream that may no longer fit your needs or desires.

Always Focus on Your Personal Growth

When it comes to developing a personal brand, personal growth is important. People who follow you are going to be genuinely engaged in your personal growth journey, regardless of what industry you are in, because your growth will inspire their growth. The more you focus on your personal growth, the more you are going to show up for and serve your audience, which allows everyone to continue growing together. Do not be afraid to endure the growth that naturally arises on your path, as well as the growth that you feel called to explore along the way, as all forms of personal growth will only help you reinforce the power of your brand.

In addition to helping your audience relate with you and feel inspired, personal growth will also help you develop a stronger brand in general. When you continually work toward personal growth, your confidence and abilities increase as well, which makes it easier for you to continue showing up and serving your audience. Not only will your increased self-confidence support your brand, but it will also support your entire life in general as you can begin enjoying more of your life and more of yourself through your personal development.

Keep Your Goals Clear

When it comes to personal branding, it can be challenging to identify what parts of yourself should be associated with your visible brand and what parts should be kept to yourself. On the one hand, you want to stay authentic and share your true self with your audience, whereas on the other hand, you want to make sure that you are not confusing them by sharing too much or getting off-brand. The best way to make sure that you are always staying on-brand with your audience is to make sure that you are clear in the goals that you have with your personal brand. If you are interested in sharing your brand with your audience so that you can teach them about marketing, then make sure that all of the parts of your personal self that you share with them in one way or another pertains to marketing. If you are developing a health and wellness brand as a personal trainer, make sure that the visible elements of your brand all coincide with your health and wellness commitments. The clearer you are with your brand development, the easier it is going to be for you to know exactly what you should be sharing, and what you should not be sharing.

In addition to having goals for your brand, do not forget to have goals for yourself, too. When it comes to developing a personal brand, it can be easy to forget that you have other aspects of your life beyond the life that you are building around your brand in the online space. Having personal goals can keep you more active in your personal life so that you can continue developing as an individual alongside developing your brand, which will further improve your chances at success.

Give Yourself Permission to Evolve

When you develop a personal brand, it can be easy to grow attached to the image that you have developed for your brand and then struggle to allow yourself to evolve over time. Many people find themselves unwilling to evolve their brand because they fear that their audience will stop following them through the changes. The reality is actually quite different: virtually every personal brand evolves over time, and in most cases, all of their loyal followers will simply evolve with them and continue to support the brand through all of the different evolutions. Some of your audience may fall off along the way, but trust that as they fall off, even more aligned members from your audience will begin arriving for you to serve them.

It is important for your overall health that you allow evolution to be a necessary staple in your brand, as no one wants to remain the same forever. Attempting to remain the same forever will cause you to lose your authenticity, which will result in your brand falling apart and you losing interest in what it is that you are trying to develop. For some business owners, this can even become a point of significant mental stress as they no longer permit themselves to be who they are, but instead attempt to remain the same in order to serve their audience. Trust that your evolution is a valuable asset to your brand, and continue working toward your evolution consistently, while also allowing it to be an important part of the brand that you are developing. The more you work together with yourself and your audience through evolution, the more authentic your brand will stay along the way.

Be Willing to Learn New Things

A part of personal development and evolution is being willing to learn new things, and this is especially important when it comes to developing a brand. When you are developing a brand, make sure that you are open to learning all of the new elements that come with the process, such as the mindset and technical strategies that are required. Do not be afraid to put yourself out there and learn a new skill if it is going to help you develop your brand faster.

At first, much of what goes into developing a brand needs to be done by you—unless you plan on hiring people to support you with everything. Even still, you should be developing your brand for you, as developing it in any other way could result in your brand not coming across as authentic or interesting. If you want to increase your chances at being recognized by your target audience, learning how to develop your social media accounts, website, and message in general is vital. Not only is this going to help you develop your brand with your message, but it also empowers you to run your brand your way so that even if you cannot afford to hire anyone for help, you can still develop all of the working parts of your brand yourself. Do not be afraid to take courses, or read books like this one, on social media marketing and the like to support you in developing your brand in the online space.

Learn to Let Go

When it comes to developing your online brand, you also need to learn to let go. Letting go may be one of the most powerful tools that you learn when it comes to developing your personal brand, as it will allow you to keep your brand moving forward even in the face of adversity. Two of the most important times that you need to pay attention to letting go is when it comes to letting go of the things mean people say, and letting go of your need to be perfect. Criticism and perfectionism are two of the more challenging things to work through when it comes to developing your business, and learning to let go is a major key for allowing you to overcome both of these things.

Many people find that having criticism toward their brand is challenging because they feel like they are being attacked personally, which is rarely true. When it comes to criticism, you need to understand that in most cases, people are only criticizing your services, not you, and they are rarely criticizing you in a way that is intended to be harsh or mean. Instead, they are simply trying to provide you with feedback, and they may not necessarily have the skills required to provide positive feedback.

When it comes to letting go of perfectionism, this strategy is a powerful way to help you get your content out there sooner, rather than later. One thing that many people do is hold themselves back because they want everything to look perfect, which is rarely important to anyone other than themselves. Attempting to hold yourself up to standards of perfectionism can lead to you being afraid to move forward with anything because you will always be looking for flaws in your work. While you want to be proud of what you do, aim to have high standards, not perfect standards. Attempting to do everything perfectly will only result in you feeling as though you are not good enough, which may lead to you feeling unworthy of running your business. Do not be afraid to let go of perfectionism so that you can develop your business to the best of your abilities, and trust that your skills will evolve and improve as you grow.

Chapter 7 Don't be too professional

Professionalism is important for making your channel look like a big deal and something worth viewing, but this shouldn't make you lose touch with reality. It is important to always stay grounded and relevant to your audience. While viewers appreciate well-produced, high quality videos, they also want the content to be relatable and fun. For instance, there are plenty of very professional business executives in the television business. These executives wear suits and look professional in every way, including their physical appearance. They also have years, sometimes decades, of experience creating well-produced and high-quality programming on television. However, most viewers today, and definitely the younger audience, will say that there is nothing that ruins a television show faster than network executives getting too involved in the production of the shows they love. To put it plainly, these executives are the perfect embodiment of professionalism but that professionalism doesn't help them relate to or understand an audience and what they want to see. It is important that no matter what level of production your channel is able to reach that you don't forget what really made you popular to begin with, and this is always going to be your content and likeability.

One of the most common criticisms of YouTube channels after they succeed is that they forget what made them popular to begin with and in a sense they sell out. While this isn't the biggest concern you need to have when your channel hasn't even become popular yet, it is important to remember when your channel does finally and hopefully takes off. Growing your channel is the first step, but you could just as easily lose all of that growth in a short amount of time if you don't remain grounded and relatable to your audience. This doesn't mean you should be unprofessional, but don't become one of the talking suits that so routinely interferes with and ruins good content in television and movies either.

Chapter 8 Facebook Marketing

The Facebook Platform

What Is Facebook?

Facebook is arguably the most famous social media platform of this age. It is basically a channel that a lot of people make use of when they want to share photos and videos. It is also a trusted way to connect with old friends.

Although the general belief is that Mark Zuckerberg created Facebook, he did not do it alone. He created the platform alongside some colleagues from Harvard, namely Andrew McCollum, Eduardo Saverin, Chris Hughes, and Dustin Moskovitz. After its creation, Facebook was launched in 2004.

Their initial plan was for it to help Harvard students communicate with each other. Sometime later, it became "a thing" in other nearby universities as well. Two years after the launch, lots of teenagers became owners of accounts on Facebook. Now, there are over a billion accounts on this website.

How Does Facebook Work?

Signing up on Facebook is very easy. You can do so from its homepage, for one. As soon as you provide answers to their personal questions and fill in your age, the next step is to find your friends among the Facebook users out there. There are various ways to go about this. You can either let the platform have access to your contact list or search for people you know by name.

Before doing the latter, though, it is essential to complete your profile. It will make it easy for your friends, family members, and acquaintances to recognize you and accept your friend request. You can post pictures, links, videos or anything you wish to share with everyone. It can be on your timeline or that of a friend. Anything you post will be visible on the news feed of your friends regardless of where you make the post.

What Is Facebook News Feed?

Facebook's News Feed comprises a collection of stories that gets updated regularly. It occupies your home page's center after logging in. Here, you will see photos, links, videos, status updates, likes, app activities, groups, and pages that your friends uploaded on the platform.

Facebook chooses the posts that appear on your feed. It is mainly dependent on your activities there, as well as the users that make up your friends list. Hence, there is a huge likelihood that you will come across stories about stuff that you have searched for in the past. They may be recommended by your friends and from the groups that you visit often. If something receives lots of likes and comments, it will appear at the top of the News Feed.

Although this feature follows a chronological order when showing posts, it does not mean that the most recent ones will be seen before the older posts. It is up to you to tweak the settings to get the type of content you want on your feed. You may rely on Facebook tutorials to achieve that as well.

Devices That Allow You to Access Facebook

Facebook is accessible on virtually every device that can connect to the internet. So, you can use tablets, smartphones, laptops, etc. The fact that Facebook can be accessed by any device that connects to the internet is truly amazing. However, even more amazing is the fact that Facebook is free. To get the best out of Facebook, merely get the Facebook app.

What Facebook Features Are Available to Users?

Marketplace

Marketplace on Facebook is similar to eBay or Craigslist. It is a section that's set aside for the purchase and sale of a commodity by account holders aged 18 years old and above.

When looking to buy goods using the marketplace, you can either look for the exact item you need or browse randomly for commodities near you. Usually, every item for sale comes with a price tag. Nevertheless, you can decide to offer to pay for something at a lower price.

On the marketplace, you can get lots of stuff, including antique vehicles, new or used clothes, etc. You can send the payment through an electronic process that doesn't require users to exit the Facebook platform.

Groups

A Facebook group is no different from a virtual forum on other sites. People with the same interests can have discussions in one about the things that they have in common.

The idea is that anyone can create a group on Facebook. There are three types of groups on Facebook. These are the open, closed, and secret groups. Each group will be explained in another section.

Town Hall

With town hall, you can stay connected to officials of your local government. You not only have the freedom to get in touch with them but also decide to follow their Facebook page. Furthermore, you can go ahead to include a constitute badge. It makes it possible for your identification as a resident in a specific district.

Messenger

If you enjoy chatting, then Facebook has a feature called Messenger that can be used to chat up individuals and groups. You can also play games and make calls with it. To access Messenger on your computer, open your profile. On the home page, click on the messages tab on the top navigation panel. It will take you to a new page where you can start a new conversation or continue a conversation with your friends.

Pages

Facebook Pages gives you the opportunity to reach more people on the platform. Its function is similar to that of the regular profiles. If an individual or a firm has a page, they can share videos, photos, links, and updates on it. Their difference is that when you share anything on a Facebook page, it is only seen by your followers. Hence, public figures, celebrities, firms, and organizations usually take advantage of this feature.

There are no restrictions on the creation of pages on Facebook. If you need to promote anything, you can make one that's dedicated to it. In case you have started a band, for instance, or you are handling a business project, you might consider creating a Facebook page. Nevertheless, for firms and celebrities, the process is merely open to their representatives.

Live Audio

The live audio feature that Facebook offers is perfectly suitable for individuals who enjoy being on air but may not have a platform yet. Anyone who connects to live audio through the feed can give feedback and share it with their Facebook contacts.

Events

Are you planning to make or attend an event? Do you want to know if any of your friends will be at a concert? Do you wish to invite people as soon as possible? Well, you don't have any reason to worry since Facebook has a dedicated feature for that.

With the platform's event section, you can discover happenings that will take place close to your location. When events are created on the platform, there are options for people to indicate if they will be attending or not. It, therefore, makes it possible for the host to come up with an effective plan for their guests. Furthermore, you can find events created by people you know.

There is no limit when it comes to the kinds of occasions you can announce on Facebook. The organization is open to everyone who has an account in the channel. Also, as the creator of an event, it is up to you to determine who can and cannot see it.

Live Video

Facebook live video is pretty much the visual counterpart of the website's live audio function. With the former, you can choose to stream a video real-time. Your fans on the page can share a link to it as well even while you are still on. They can also react and comment on it as the video plays.

Thus, Facebook live video is an ideal setting for question-and-answer segments with your fans. You can also decide to ante up the streaming experience by adding stickers and even scribbling on your video.

Creating a Facebook Account

On Facebook, there are two types of accounts you can create: a personal profile or fan/business page. Below are some tips when creating such accounts.

Facebook Profile

Of the two types of Facebook accounts, the most common is the Facebook profile. It is ideal for individuals who use the platform for leisure purposes.

With a personal profile, you can post everything you want, e.g., details about your workplace or the institutions you have attended. You may also connect with people that you met a long time ago.

There is no difficulty in coming up with this account type. The registration is no different from the process that you have carried out on other platforms in the past. You merely have to provide the following information:

- First and last name
- Email and phone number
- Desired password
- Gender and date of birth

As soon as these data are correctly filled, you can click on the "Create an Account" button.

Personalizing Your Facebook Profile

If you are looking to personalize your profile on Facebook, there are procedures you can follow.

1. Select a profile picture that will represent who you are on Facebook. Adding one makes it easy for everyone to recognize you and contact you.

2. Go ahead and look for friends. You can search for friends on Facebook using their name, email ID or mobile number.

3. You can decide who can access your Facebook profile by making it private. When you have an account on the platform, after all, you are naturally putting Facebook in charge of your personal information. Hence, it is vital to set boundaries from the beginning by changing things up on Settings.

At this point, you can now interact with your acquaintances and friends. You can also receive notifications about events happening around you.

Facebook Page

Apart from having a personal account on Facebook, you can have a professional page that can also serve as your online store. There are two options available here.

Brand or Business

It is a method that ensures an increase in your business' online reach. It will help you get noticed by more potential customers.

Public Figure or Community

You can also open a Facebook community where you can make your interests known. It is an ideal way to get music, sports news, show updates, and other forms of content out in public.

To start, you need to open a personal Facebook account. The business page varies from the latter, however, because you have to be careful in selecting a suitable name so that your prospective clients can find you easily.

Once done, you have to select an excellent profile picture and cover photo. You may add details about your products as well if you intend to run a store online.

Mistakes on Facebook

Running a business page or group on Facebook means you will need to run some ads on the platform. If you fail to follow the guidelines on the platform, Facebook will not let you run any ad. Your ads may perform poorly if you don't set it up correctly.

Before running a Facebook ad campaign, it is crucial to know how to advertise on the platform. For instance, you should learn about policies that may affect the approval of your advertisements, as well as mistakes that you might make due to your inexperience. It will also be helpful to read about other successful advertisers on the platform to know how they function.

Numerous opportunities for business growth appear when you open a Facebook account. Establish your authority and enhance your organic reach with this free platform.

Strategies for Your Posts

Facebook is fundamentally based on posts and their ability to go 'viral' – which means that your content has to be so encapsulating that it draws people in. Here are some strategies for viral Facebook posts:

Use Emotions

Facebook is not really about selling products – it's about actually connecting with people. You can't connect with people unless you are selling emotions. It doesn't really matter what your product is — on Facebook, if you want people to care about your page and your brand, you have to connect with them emotionally.

The only way you can connect with people is by associating the utility of your product with things that make people relate to it. So, if you're trying to sell, say clothes, you can't just show people what you offer and hope that they wear it. If you instead put up a story of how your clothes are made and showcase the people who work endlessly to ensure that the clothes you make are perfect, you're far more likely to gain public attention.

Don't Overdo It

Of course, trying to connect with your potential audience is important, but make sure that you're not trying too hard. If you latch on to every new trend and joke around too much, it's eventually going to saturate your audience. Also, many brands think they can connect to the younger generation by using their slang and style, but try not to partake in silly things like this. It's only going to make your posts seem fake, and as though you're trying to be relatable just for the sake of it.

It's important to remember that you're selling something, at the end of the day. If you're going to try your hardest to make it seem otherwise, it's only going to make your audience unreactive to what you have to say.

Keep Posts Short & Specific

The one key element of Facebook marketing is to keep your customer's attention – if your customer sees posts that are too long, or if your all your posts are videos, they're not going to engage a lot.

Be direct with your audience and tell them what you're selling, while trying to connect with them at the same time. Most brands tend to have far more success with shorter posts than they do with huge advertising campaigns.

If you do decide to make longer posts, remember to add pictures and paragraphs. This will at least make your audience interested enough to continue reading.

Facebook Strategies

When it comes to setting up a killer page on Facebook, it is important to make it as interesting for your audience as you can. You must put in the effort to make it look as professional as possible, as well, to help your audience connect with it more effectively.

Here are some strategies that you can employ to make your Facebook page entertaining for your audience:

Personality

It is important for you to add a certain amount of personality to your Facebook page. People should be drawn in by it and feel the urge to like or comment on your content. If you settle for something mediocre, then it will not work in your favor. A good idea is to hire professionals who are good at molding pages and making them interesting for the audience. Instruct them to review your target audience and prepare an analysis of their general characteristics. Doing so helps in preparing a fitting schedule that will make your page popular. You can also look at the strategies that other companies are employing and come up with a plan that is in keeping with the same. However, it is best to maintain a little originality and remain true to your company's policies.

It pays to have a good sense of who you are and what your company stands for. If you remain confused, this will work against you. It is best to develop an image that you would like to portray and then pursue the same. Remember that things can look like one thing in your mind and another on paper. So it is best to create a page and ensure it looks exactly like you planned it.

Consistency

Remember that consistency is key. You have to be consistent with your posts, and they should be coherent. Your Facebook page should be a slice of your store and the products you sell there. Don't make it too different, as this can confuse your customers. If you have a team working for you, instruct them to post content at regular intervals and not keep the audience waiting. A good trick is to know when people prefer to see an update come their way and schedule your content to publish during those times. But don't make it boring, as you want to keep your audience engaged. Again, you can look at a successful company's strategy and come up with a posting schedule that suits your own business. As mentioned earlier, it is best to aim for the early evening slot, as that's when most people are active online.

Frequency

When it comes to maintaining an online profile for your company, it is extremely important to update often. You must try to schedule new posts at regular intervals so people know what to expect and when to expect them. A golden rule is to post in the evenings, as that is when most people expect new content. Try to increase the frequency of the posts as and when the company grows. Some companies prefer to post new posts thrice a day, as that helps in keeping the audience glued. But it is important not to get carried away and post too many things all at once. You cannot overload the audience with too much information, as it will end up confusing them. Keep the information relevant and coherent. You can always do a short trial and error to see what is working for you and what isn't. For example, you can ask your audience how often they would like to receive an email from you. If they are happy with the frequency, you can maintain it, or change it according to their preferences.

Business Goals

It is quite important to be in sync with your business goals and update your page from time to time by keeping in mind your main motivations. Your page should be a thorough representation of your company speaking to your ambitions and portraying your true intentions. It pays to incorporate a little of your company's policies in every new post.

Converting your Profile to a Business Page

If you already have a Facebook profile and wish to convert it into a page without creating a separate one, you can do so easily. Here are some simple instructions:

At the top right-hand corner of your Facebook profile, you will find a drop-down button. Under that, you will find "manage pages", which gives you the option to "create a page." Click here, and you will be able to add a page to your current profile. There, you will be able to automatically convert your current profile into a page.

You can also merge your profile with your page. Click settings and download a copy of your Facebook page, then select the profile to page migration option. Remember, once it is merged, you won't be able to retrieve your profile. You have to make up your mind before making the transition. To merge your business page, go to settings, choose the general tab, and select either the merge pages and merge duplicate pages, then choose the pages that you want to merge. But remember, the two pages have to be identical — including same exact address and information — otherwise, they will not merge into one.

It is easier to create a brand-new page dedicated to your company. However, you will have to fill in all the different details from scratch.

Merchandize

It is a good idea to start with the merchandise. This includes offering exclusive goods that are not available at the store. For example, you can offer a new product that people can only buy through your Facebook page or website and not at the store. Alternately, you can offer a customized product that is exclusively available online. Say, for example, you offer to customize a product to the customer's liking by changing the color scheme or encrypting a message, etc. You can also offer a product in a color scheme or pattern that is different from whatever is available in the store. Make it obvious by posting appropriate announcements and tell your customers they are online exclusives. You can also tell the people in your store to check it out online in order to direct their attention to your Facebook page.

Offers

You can run exclusive online offers, as well. These can include schemes such as buy one get one free, or get a complimentary gift, etc. Such offers are sure to generate interest and enhance your page's value. Again, it is important to advertise, so people are made aware of the offer. You can send out emails detailing the same and tell people about the offers you have made available to your online audience. You can also advertise it in your store or hand out flyers to people, encouraging them to visit your Facebook page.

Rewards

You can reward people who bring in a specific number of likes, too. This works well as people will be prompted to bring in more and more potential new customers to like your page. The reward needs to be a little appealing in order to capture your audience's interest. You can offer coupons, free merchandise, or specially-designed merchandise. All of these will prove to be quite appealing and help lure in more people to like your page. You can make an announcement on the page as well as on your other social media accounts. You can also mention it on your website and inform the people who visit your physical store.

Discount coupons

You can offer discount coupons and discounts to your customers. These coupons will allow them to pay a lower amount for the products and services that you have on offer in your store. They will be able to avail these coupons only on the Facebook page. Again, you must announce it on all your social media accounts, such as Twitter and Instagram, to inform people.

Contests

Contests are a fun way to get people to visit your page. These help people get involved in an exciting way. The contest should be related to the products or services that you offer, like adding a tagline or completing a phrase or posting pictures of the products. You can announce the contest on your Facebook page, and ensure that you also announce a good prize that will excite people enough to partake in the contest. Setting a short deadline is a must, as you will have the chance to increase your page views in a short period of time.

Events

You can also announce events, where people can meet up and get to know each other better. Such events will also help you know your own audience. You can organize food and drinks, as well.

Events can help you out a lot if they are done correctly. All you have to do is create an interesting event, invite as many people as you can, and spread awareness with the help of your page. The benefit from this is that you don't have to spend a ton of money sponsoring events organized by other people — a lot of people sponsor local events to get name recognition.

However, you can use Facebook to gain name recognition without spending a lot of money through events. Events can become very well-known if they are publicized in the right way. First, you'll need to identify the kind of event that your target audience would be interested in. Once you have done that, start inviting people and spread the word about the event.

Say you are a local bakery who wants name recognition in your locality. Start by thinking of a creative event you can use to publicize your business while also giving your customers a fun time. Create a related event on Facebook and start inviting people that you know are in your area; use your contacts as well as your Facebook page. Use the event to promote your company, and keep publicizing your bakery so that your small business gets name recognition.

This is just the start — by spending a little more money, you can create events that will attract thousands of people. Start slowly with events that won't require a significant investment, and once you see that the events are helping streamline revenue, you can start expanding to bigger events to get even more name recognition.

These are just some of the different offers you can run online, and are not limited to just these. You can modify them all to suit your company's policies.

Reasons Why You Should Use Facebook Advertising

You have seen how you can use Facebook for your business, now let's look at the reasons why you should use Facebook for advertising.

1. Facebook advertising is extremely effective. Because of how many people are on Facebook, it's hard to ignore that Facebook is a major part of everyone's life. In fact, Facebook is considered to be one of the top advertising channels online because digital ads make up 51% of total advertising in the United States.

2. Simple set up and fast results. Setting up a Facebook campaign is going to take very little time and will provide you with excellent results. Digital advertising produces terrific ROI and will be extremely fast when you assign the best campaign strategy with the best product that you have to offer. Facebook has the tools to help you drive traffic to your website and even allows you to boost single posts.

3. You can reach the perfect audience. You have already seen how you can design the perfect clientele that will help you when it comes to targeting the right demographic. It's also going to make your advertising more successful.

4. Facebook campaigns are customizable. You'll be able to create the perfect ad experience because it will only be seen by your specified audience choice. All of this is made possible because of the different ad formats that Facebook provides you when you create your ad campaigns.

5. Facebook adds new features every month. Because of how adaptive Facebook is your ads will constantly evolve to reach the perfect audience.

6. You can set your own budget on Facebook which is going to allow you to advertise for as little as $1. Even though this is a small budget, your campaign is still going to reach a lot of people.

7. You can easily track your performance and ROI with the analytic tools that Facebook provides such as your ad manager.

8. You'll get an edge over your competitors because not everyone is using Facebook, or they are not using it properly. therefore, you're going to gain an advantage over your competition. So, exploit it while you can!

9. Facebook is compelling with regards to push going back and forth leads down the pipeline. This strategy will work for any marketer that is trying to

target their clients that have already visited your website which means that they are most likely going to be attracted to your business on some level.

10. Facebook makes it easy for you to find new leads. As you saw earlier, you'll have the tools with Facebook business manager that will let you look at people who are interested in specific hobbies or certain pages that will lead you to more people who could be interested in your business but have yet to hear about you.

Facebook Pixel

So, what is Facebook Pixel? A lot of people tend to forget about Facebook Pixel because the internet is filled with cookies. Cookies will track the movements of your website visitors. In the end, Pixels are just the same as cookies.

Facebook Pixel Functions

Pixels have multiple actions that will aid you while you're creating your marketing campaigns.

1. Track conversions: Conversions will be any action that your visitors complete. Facebook Pixel is able to keep track of 9 different types of conversions that will be available to you in order for you to improve your conversion rate and targeting. Take for example, you're running a campaign that costs $1

per click and get up to 500 clicks. Pixel is going to be able to tell you exactly how many people clicked on the ad and how it's actually converted.

2. Optimize ads for conversions: One of the biggest differences between Google Analytics and Facebook Pixel will be how Facebook uses the information collected by Pixel. Instead of just showing you what is seen, Facebook will collect the data and then target people who are similar to those that are already being converted. Therefore, by optimizing your targeting which will help to improve your chances for success.

3. Retargeting ads: Online, retargeting will be when you send ads to those that have already shown an interest in your site or have interacted with you before. Facebook's Pixels will allow you to retarget people who have performed a specific action on your website.

Take for instance, if you visit an airline website to search for trips, you'll notice that once you leave the site, there will be more ads that are related to traveling. You're not imagining this. You're being targeted so they can get you to spend money on their site.

Most marketers know that retargeting customers will be easier to convert because they have already visited your site. That means that they are more likely to become a normal customer.

Creating a Facebook Pixel

Facebook Pixel can sound scary, but it's a lot easier to do than you think. Here we will go through the steps to creating a Facebook Pixel.

1. Enter your ad account and select the menu choice. From this point you should go to "all tools" which is going to expand the menu. You'll then click on "Pixel" which can be found under measure and report.

2. Facebook will then prompt you to create your own Pixel.

3. The only thing that you're going to need to do is provide a name for your Pixel. The name is not going to be public therefore you can name it something that is logical to you.

4. You'll be required to accept the terms of conditions.

5. Now you'll click on the option that will give you a new menu. When adding Pixel to your website, a lot of people decide to manually install it, or you can email the instructions to a developer if that is easier for you.

6. Last, you'll copy the code that is provided and add it to your website.

If this is the case, you'll want to use the integration or tag manager option rather than manually install the code yourself one.

From there you're going to click on the Shopify icon and then copy the integration code that is provided.

Adding Pixel to WordPress or Shopify

There are a couple of different methods that can be used in order to add Pixel to your website.

1. Direct upload to WordPress. Follow these simple steps in order to install Pixel.

x. Go to your WordPress dashboard and click on the left menu. From there you'll click on appearance and editor.

y. file. On the right-hand side you'll move to theme files, you'll scroll down till you see the theme header or header.php. You're now going to be able to edit your WordPress theme's header

z. Scroll down until you can see the closing head tag.

aa. Add in a few blank lines between the closing head tag and any code before it. Now you'll insert the Pixel code to the new blank lines.

bb. Save your file and upload it with an FTP program.

Note: When you decide to change your theme, you'll have to go through this process again because Pixel will be removed from the theme changes.

2. Through a WordPress plugin. This is recommended when you're inserting headers and footers. But there are a variety of plugins that you can use if you want.

cc. From the left menu, choose plugins and add new.

dd. Use your search on the lower right side in order to find the plugin you want to use.

ee. Install and activate the header and footer plugin to your website.

ff. Now move back to your menu and choose settings before clicking on insert headers and footers.

gg. open your plugin and search for scripts in header before pasting the Pixel code in the proper box.

hh. Save and refresh your page.

One of the best benefits when it comes to this plugin is that when you change themes, your Pixel is still going to be on your website.

Note: If you're using Pixel on one website, you can install the Facebook Pixel helper which is located on Chrome. This is going to allow you to see any events that are happening in real time.

    3. Shopify direct upload. This method should only be utilized if you feel comfortable updating your site's theme.

ii.   Got Shopify and click on the online store.

jj.   On your new menu you'll click on themes.

kk.   In the themes section you'll click on actions and then click on edit code.

ll.   Under the layout folder you'll need to click on the theme that you're currently using.

mm.   Scroll down until you see the closing head tag.

nn.   Make sure you add in a few lines before the head tag and any code that comes before it. You'll then enter your Pixel code into these blank lines.

oo.   Click save.

    4. Shopify integration. Since some people are not comfortable when it comes to editing code, Shopify has created a simpler method so you don't have to mess with any of the code.

pp.		Go to Shopify and click on the online store off the left-hand side menu.

qq.		In your new menu, select preferences.

rr.		ON this new page, move down until you see a box that asks you about your Pixel id.

ss.		Paste your Pixel id into the box.

tt.		Save your new changes.

Installing and using Pixel may end up being the most effective marketing strategy that you'll decide to use. It's only going to be a few steps that you have to follow in order to have access to powerful analytics on your website.

Creating High-Quality Facebook Content for Your Audience

If you want to keep increasing the number of visitors on your Facebook page or group, you need to be consistent with the content that you offer. You will gain their interest and promote engagement if you always provide high-quality content.

Here are some steps you can follow to create noteworthy Facebook posts for your audience.

Change Up the Content You Upload

Don't make the content you publish appear monotonous. It's not every time your audience will be interested in reading a long post. Sometimes, having a photo gallery to scroll through is beneficial as well. You should create a balance between the following types of contents:

Press Releases

These should contain information regarding changes in your business policies, service improvements, and general updates.

Blog Posts

Articles should provide details that will benefit your customers or describe anything new that goes on with the business.

Videos

They may consist of how-to, motivational, and other types of beneficial videos.

Photos

You can upload pictures of your products, office building, workers, or events.

Let Your Fans Contribute to the Wall

When you want to attract a specific audience, the Facebook page should become your fan page. It will be incomplete if your visitors don't have the option of posting directly on your wall. To promote engagement with your customers and fans, therefore, make sure to have this feature enabled. If you are unsure how to do that, you may check your settings.

Always Captivate Your Audience

The quality or relevance of your content will not matter if your presentation is boring. You must showcase it in a way that interests your audience.

If your business is in the gaming sector, for instance, your viewers will stop going through posts, considering they only tell them how to clean their consoles or maintain their accessories. Why don't you have a top ten review or pick the best games you have played instead? You don't have to be an expert at it; you can share your opinions on the games that you wish to recommend.

Professionalism may not be the best option when running a business on Facebook. A lot of times, you will need to be able to interact at the same level as your target audience. This can show them how important they are to you.

Leave a Question After Each Post to Promote Interaction

Everyone wants the post they see to feel personal. Your visitors will not feel the need to comment on it if there is no question to prompt a response from them.

To entice people to interact and leave a comment on your page, you should add questions after every post. A call to action is another alternative to promote engagement on the page as well.

Now, depending on what your post covers, there are numerous questions you may ask. If you uploaded a video on "tips for smoother skin," for instance, you can encourage your viewers to comment about their personal experience with the tips or share other suggestions on how to smoothen the skin. Remember: a good question is all you need to start an excellent conversation with potential consumers.

Align Your Content with Your Audience's Interests

It is easy to get comfortable with posting content that only relates to your business. After all, you are running your brand's page or group. However, you should also provide information that will be beneficial to your customers.

If you sell athletic shoes, for example, then you are sure that most - if not all - of your consumers focus on fitness. Sharing some videos with excellent workout tips, therefore, may be appreciable for them. If customers know that they can rely on you to get information, it can help to solidify your relationship.

Don't Oversaturate the News Feed

When you want a large number of people to notice your page, you may consider uploading a lot of posts to get their attention. If you are already halfway through this door, it is advisable for you to step out.

The reason is that many Facebook users will block you quickly if their newsfeed is getting filled up with your posts alone. You are not giving them any room to view feeds from their friends and family on the platform.

If you want your content to get more attention, you should have a regular day and time when you upload them. If you stay consistent with the quality of the posts, your audience will look forward to the days when you will be publishing them.

Tailor Your Posts to Suit the Facebook Platform

With so many social media platforms available, each one has some aspects that make them unique. Say, on Twitter, the '#' and '@' are the symbols that appear frequently. While most Twitter users understand what they represent, a lot of Facebook users may not. Hence, you are lifting one of your posts off Twitter, it is necessary to edit the post to suit Facebook's standard. You don't want to cause a misunderstanding between you and your audience, after all.

Promote Creativity Through Your Contests

Since fan pages commonly host contests, you need to be creative to make yours stand out. The online competitions you hold may come with a video, photo or essay entry. To promote creativity, you can ask your customers to come up with costume, logo or art designs, as well as articles that you may post on your blog or website.

If a participant submits an entry, remember to tag your customers when uploading it on your page. By doing so, the post will show up on their wall and become visible to their friends and followers. It is an easy way to reach more Facebook users.

Don't Get Carried Away by Hosting Contests

When building a great fan page, hosting contests play a vital role in your success. Any competition you host should excite your audience and turn into a fun activity for the participants. Nevertheless, keep in mind that their effectiveness will dwindle if you host them too often.

A good strategy to use when scheduling contests is to choose dates close to an upcoming event. Having an Easter egg hunt during the Easter season, for instance, will help get them into the Easter mood.

Choose One Topic for a Month

Having a unique topic to cover in a month is a great way to keep your audience interested. In addition to the posts that you will upload on your page, you also need to add links to other sites where your viewers can get more information about the topic.

If all your content revolve around a single subject, your viewers will quickly lose interest in them. Besides, you are likely to run out of exciting things to talk about by doing so. When you provide various topics, though, you can expand your target audience.

Get a handle on success today. Start publishing high-quality content that will captivate and engage your audience as much as possible.

Understanding the Facebook Group

Creating Facebook Group

The process of creating a Facebook group is quite simple. Since you already have a personal profile, you can create the group using the same account. The first step is to view the options in the drop-down menu on the top right corner of the Facebook page. You will find the "Create Group" tab there along with the logout and activity log buttons.

The next step is to decide on a name for the group that you are creating. It is essential for it to be similar to that of your existing business if it is in relation to that. By going with this option, your customers from another platform can find you with ease.

Then, you have to invite people to become members of the group. There are different means of doing so.

The first option is to find the individuals you want to find on Facebook and then send an invite to these users. The interested ones will join the group by accepting the invitation. Another option is to forward a group invite to the email address of the users. Getting the latter information should not be an issue since it is standard for most businesses. You can invite members at any time since you will be running the group as an administrator.

After completing the steps above, your next task is to pick the group type.

- Secret groups
- Closed groups
- Public groups

A secret group is not visible to other Facebook users. It is not possible to find it if you are not a member. The things posted on this group are exclusive as well.

The closed group is quite similar to the secret group. Unlike the secret groups, all Facebook users can search for the community and view details of the members. Only the content posted on the group remains private.

The last and most common type you will find is the public group. It refers to online communities that do not require someone to become a member before viewing the posts there.

Selecting a Group Icon

Another area to consider when creating the group is choosing a group icon. The icon will appear in different ways at the side of the group name. It is necessary to make your group stand out since it appears along with the group name in a search result.

Chapter 9 Instagram Marketing

Instagram Contents

As stated earlier, Instagram is a platform that works by visuals posts. Everything shared are either photos, graphics or videos. Because of this, very many people find it hard to create contents; many don't even know how to post or whether a posting is allowed. Those that know these are confused on what sort of content should be on Instagram. In this section, you will be taken through the parts of the content, types of contents and processes of creating content on Instagram. Attention is paid keenly to direct you through crafting perfect posts.

Because of the nature of the platform, visuals and branded storytelling are the keys of contents used. To engage your followers as a business-oriented person, telling a story about your product and services is the key to being the best seller. Posting pictures that are 'meaningless' will never add anything to your account. On Instagram, create a story that will be of great impact to your followers and any potential ones. The best thing to do is to put your gaze on your followers. You must, with utmost clarity, put them into consideration because they are the one to be engaged. Be adroit in your post to ensure entertainment and genuine contents. Be skillful in the way you arrange your photos. While uploading the photos, show them the nature of people in support of your business, the type of person you are, the muse of your story, and lots more. Don't take the time of your audience; make the story succinct and exclusive to Instagram news only. Be dynamic in the chronological arrangement of the stories. To ensure uniqueness of your profile, make sure you are updated on the latest trends on the platform. These trends could be news or hashtags, write on them and use them as well. Devise a way of connecting your interesting contents in such a way that your followers will have to stay on your profile to get the full story. Get the interaction with them interesting; they will surely look up for more. There are some basic things to consider while constructing a good Instagram content. These, according to Martins, are:

The Right time

You have to skillfully detect the right time to post your story based on your targeted audience. You must be up-to-date on their personal activities. Note that on your newsfeed, the most recent posts receive more attention which is why your post must be timely. You must key into an opportunity such as this. According to Martin "if your viral page is aimed at students who are online in the morning, then you should post in this period." This means the free time which your targeted audience is likely to be free to check their Instagram should be considered before posting. He gave another example that if you have 9-to5-jobbers as a target group, then you should write more posts after work. These people will have free time randomly; by this, you must post in their timing too. He, however, gave a recommendation which is not 'convenient test' as generally 7-9 clock (breakfast), 11-14 clock (lunch) and 17 to 20 clock (after work). The best interaction on Instagram was also given as 17-18 clock. The time frame of your location should not affect your audience consideration. Although most times, you and your followers are in the same meridian.

The Picture

Instagram can also be referred to as an electronic photo album. This is because it contains much of them. The pictures to be posted must be very attractive. Consider editing your photos before uploading them. Make sure the post is dynamic with different types of things such as comedy videos, photos and all. Try to upload pictures that are showing the practical time people are consuming your product. Research has it that many people consider photos from real life scenes of the product as the authenticity of the product. High-quality photos are recommended; make sure you don't post low-quality photos and videos. Be dynamic in the selection and arrangement of the pictures. Make sure you include a brand of your company on a photo that is not really related. Don't let your followers have bad impressions about you. If you make necklaces, consider using your friends as part of the models and then take their pictures for onward uploads on to your account. Take pictures of people that have worn the necklace to events such as weddings to authenticate it. Being outstanding should be your goal by creating compelling contents that entertain people. The type of pictures you will post for children will be different from the adults'. You must do all your best to get their target at different times as well. You should catch their attention at once sometimes too. The arrangement of your pictures also matters. The recommended arrangement is the grid formula. With a grid, you have the opportunity to arrange your pictures chronologically to explain the story you are telling. Apart from this, followers can quickly trace the story effortlessly. The posts must be able to hold anyone that runs across the posts; they must locate your account and follow.

The Text

Even though Instagram is basically visual, texts could be added to it sometimes too. Most times, these texts should be one that will require the action of the followers. The texts should vary between lengthy words and short ones. The place your company is located will be an additional text for you in cases you don't know the text to use. The aim is to engage your followers. Your text must be relevant to your pictures and most times should be one or two words. When you include your location, the post will be expanded to reach more audience thereby popularizing the account –this is your goal. Make sure the text is proofread, don't spoil the mind of the people that are already interested in you. Text can be a statement on the images uploaded as well. With this, if you are uploading pictures that are not a direct replica of your product, many of your followers will understand vividly.

Best steps to creating audience-centered contents

Having a business account requires the consistent engagement of your audience. This makes good contents an unavoidable thing to be included in your profile. You can consider the following tricks given by Instagram influencer Christina Galbato when creating a laudable content:

Use ready-made templates tools

When you want to create contents on Instagram and wonder how to create a pattern for them or perhaps stumbled on a great profile with nice and cool contents, and you want to create, template tools is what top Instagram influencers used. There are lots of tools Canva, Venngage and Adobe with great Spark posts. These tools will craft an outstanding content that titillates the eyes and leave the mind wondering what sort the pictures is. You don't need to stress yourself, search for any of these tools, insert your pictures and you will be wowed by the outcome. It has trial sections, and you can equally choose manually that template you love.

- *Research and Use High-quality stock images*

That you will need lots of images is a fact. On the contrary, stock images could be awkward on your news-feed. Be extremely careful while using it most especially with templates. Everyone needs varying images to be created as contents, visit Stocksnap.io or Un-splash for free nice images. If you are buoyant enough, you could log onto Stocksy for images with high quality, different niche pictures, etc. Stocksy provides the greatest images because it is paid for and the developers want it to be worth it. Bear in mind that the standard pixel for images to be uploaded as content on Instagram is 1080p X 1080p to avoid automatic image resolutions. Stock images are always great and nice because the sites where they are found were actually developed to meet the criteria of social platforms such as Instagram.

Vary your content's format

Dynamism is the way forward in having a good followers' turn up on your content. You can't be deaf to the reaction of the followers when creating your contents. You could create a short video, say of 1-minute duration, explaining your product or showing the practical usage of your product. Don't bore your viewers with just a single type of pictures; it could be extremely boring really. A good Instagram profile will house varying contents. The distinction in the contents is only in their format. Take your time to create GIF contents as well. You could have a picture, GIF and short video and their permutation as well. This is what your audience is expecting, give them. Though Instagram takes both GIF and Videos as the same thing, GIF is always shorter but interactive. Lots of people expect it as well. Stuff your contents with a variety of formats.

Search for brands within your niche and repost them

Perhaps creating contents yourself is barely possible because of time constraints. Don't worry; there is a way out of the tunnel. You can, with the consent of the writer, report a post within your niche from another content writer. Example of posts you could repost are those posts from fast-growing Instagram users. They must be of interest to your audience though. However, on Instagram, there are special steps to go through in order to make reposting official –reposting without proper consultation could lead to offense. Follow the steps below:

1. Follow hashtags and accounts to find out quality content

In order to validate your reposting, ensure that you have a similar audience and brand. Make the person you want repost his/her content is not a direct competitor to you. Make sure you have proper thinking on the content as well. You must follow the person in order to be updated on the posts of the person. To save the contents you would love to repost, try to create a collection for easy access. Searching for related contents through hashtag is also a legal way.

2. Contact the user for permission to repost

Before asking for permission, make sure you let the writer know they are doing a great job with proper credit and that your audience will be interested in the same post. To ask for permission, send the writer a DM through the arrow beneath the picture. Using the arrow has proven most efficient way, according to the report, of sending a direct message to account users.

3. Share the picture on your news feed

You can now share the picture to your feed once the permission has been granted. You must make sure proper credit is given to the source of the post anyway.

4. Save the Photo from Instagram or share directly through the repost feature

There are two ways of reposting on Instagram: saving from Instagram and reposting directly. For the first one, you will need to find the picture, click on the photo, double click it, view page source, type jpg there, copy the URL of the first option, open a new browser, paste it there, right click and save the picture. On the second option, copy the URL of the post you like and click on "repost" and it will automatically repost it. Note that the watermark is maintained when you use the second option. The first looks complex likewise, try to accompany the process given with required practical.

Create a UGC Campaign

The acronym UGC means 'User Generated Content.' It is used as content created by your followers. You could be the initiator, and they could post within your niche. This is also an activity similar to reposting of contents. User-generated content is typically contents crafted by any product user on their products without encouragement from anyone. These are contents solicited by you from your followers, though most times with incentives to encourage them. You can involve your followers in different ways: selling your product at a discount rate, conducting a competition on creating a post on your brand, etc. Instagram has suggested that you announce your hashtag even on other platforms especially the part of the incentives. Be strategic and dynamic in your request for contents from your audience. Without dynamism in your request, your feed will always be the same thing which will bore your audience. If you stipulate too many rules are guiding the kind of post you want, you might end up with no post as many people might be afraid they won't be considered. Relying too much on your followers is not a good idea as well. Make sure their posts are just supplementary and not the main thing. Proof to them you can actually create your content yourself and create a feeling that their support is a means to encourage them only.

Do influencer collaboration

One fantastic thing to do to create a good audience-centered profile is to work with other great brand promoters too. This will get you new followers, great feed and many other things enjoyed by the person you collaborated with. You must ensure the collaboration is with someone within your own niche to avoid exploitation and misunderstanding. Worry less on how to contact top influencers as many of them have a contact in their bio basically for collaboration inquiries purpose.

You have learned how to create good content for your brand and business. However, note that whatever means you are using to get your contents, designing will surely be done by you. Because of this, you will need to learn basic tricks used by top influencers to design their contents. These tricks are:

- ✓ *Stating a precise focal point*

While uploading your pictures and creating your format, make sure your photo has focus. The focus of photos means the center where you want your viewers to pay their attention only. If you create a picture with lots of images on, you might lose the focus, affecting its effect on the viewers. Therefore, put a single image with many other things, if need be, pointing only to the central idea of the photo.

- ✓ *Adhere to the rule of thirds*

The rule of thirds, found in photography, is all about arranging your interesting features along with a 9-grid picture intersection. This rule is a classic rule and executed by 9-grid photo imagination. Make sure that in uploading many pictures on your profile, you must adhere strictly to this rule –it is the secret of the top influencers. With amazing third rule obedience, you will adjust your grid to one-third of the picture you wish to upload as well.

✓   *Create and apply white space and borders*

Creating space and borders around your photos gives it a compelling look, and the audience will always want to gaze more. To avoid jam-packed uploads, ensure that you maintain some space between your third rule and focal point picture. Make sure you add this effect to all your posts, and you will experience rapid growth of followers.

✓   *Rapt attention should be to Contrast and balance*

Give your picture a good contrast while uploading. The contrast of your picture ranges over its color, light, shape, fonts, white space and border, and lots more. To ensure you have a perfect contrast setting, you could play around the various types of it on your Instagram app. Contrast is an important part of content designed to highly engage your audience. Many people are fascinated by the enhancement of a given picture even before focusing on the content itself. Contrast is like a finishing effect that 'crowns' your effort in content design. This is the last stage of content design, make sure it counts, and you will be amazed by the number of turn out your account will experience.

Using Instagram Live

Why Use Instagram Live for Business?

Just like you would use stories, it is important to use Instagram Live for your business. Not only can it be a great channel for connecting with your audience and increasing followers, but also going after business goals and generating leads. It can also help you get discovered better on Instagram.

Just like Instagram stories, making interesting Instagram Live videos can help you show up on the explore page that can make it easier to find you. It will be easier to broadcast your message and connect better with your audiences.

Instagram Live can be quite flexible as you get to decide what to broadcast and offer workshops, and answer questions etc.

You can make it fun and engaging for your audience to hold their attention.

How to Use Instagram Live for Business

Just like stories, Instagram Live can be used as an easy tool to broadcast a live video. Here are some things to keep in mind:

Viewers

You get to choose who to broadcast live to. You do not have to do it for all, and select only a few to broadcast to. You can choose to hide it from specific accounts by selecting the "Hide Story From" option.

Moderating Comments

As you know, when you go live, you allow people to comment on your video and you will not have control over what they say. If you wish to avoid any language that is inappropriate, then it is best to go to the settings and find "Comments" and go to "Hide Inappropriate Comments" and turn it from off to on. You can add custom keywords that you wish to appear in the comments.

Setting up a Live Broadcast

- Start by swiping right on the home screen or the camera icon on the top left to access the camera.

- Choose the "Live" camera option and "Start Live Video" option. If your notifications are off, then your audience might not be notified when you go live so make sure you switch on notifications.

- The number of people viewing will appear on the top and their comments at the bottom.

- Once done, touch the "End" button in the top right corner and "End Live Video."

Instagram Ads and Ad Budget

When it comes to creating ads for Instagram, it is important to use the right tools to create appealing ads. Here are some types of ads you can choose to make for your products:

Photo Ads

Single image ads help to create about six ads that contain an image each.

- To create them, start by choosing the images you wish to use in the ads.
- Go through the library and upload pictures or choose free stock images.
- Add the caption you would want to use for the ad in the text field.
- The caption can be 300 characters long with the third line having ellipsis that will make the audience click on expand to view it fully.
- It is ideal to choose 125 characters for ads as otherwise it can be burdening.
- You can add a website link or a URL.
- You do not have to fill out all the fields such as the display link, headline, link description etc.
- Go to advanced options to change pixels or advanced tracking.

Video Ads

Single video ads are comprised of a video or a gif.

- To create them, go to the video thumbnail and add a video from your gallery or shoot one.
- Upload one that runs for 15 seconds for best results.
- If you wish to caption the video, then use an SRT file.
- It is best to add captions using 125 characters just as in the case of photo ads. Again, limit it to 125 characters.

Slideshow Ads

Slideshow ads are nothing but video ads that play on loop and can have 10 images with music supplementing it.

- To create them, go to the library and create a slideshow using the creator.
- Add the images and then arrange them to your liking and adjust the settings. Add in music if you like by choosing the icon on the top right.

Carousel Ads

Carousel ads are made up of images and videos.

- To make them, create cards for the ads. You can add up to 10 cards at a time.

- Add in headline or caption or text to each of the cards.

- You can choose to leave the description empty or add a URL.

- Add lead forms as it makes for an important step of the process.

- Regardless of the ad format you choose, create your lead form.

- If you already have one, then you can use the same or make a new one for the ads.

- If you wish to make one, then the fields to fill out includes the welcome screen, headline, image, layout, button text, questions, privacy policy, and thank you screen etc.

- A website link can also be added.

- Once done, click on the finish button.

- Once you click on it, you will not be able to edit it.

How Much Does it Cost?

How much the ads will cost will depend on the budget you set for it and whether you wish to use the manual or automatic bidding system.

As per marketing experts, running your ads on Instagram will be almost twice as cost-effective as running them on other social media platforms such as Facebook.

Although it is difficult to assess how much an ad can cost, it is safe to assume that the ad can be around $5. This is half of what it takes to come up with Facebook ads that can be around $10.

Don't worry about your budget going bust, as you will hardly ever over-shoot it when making Instagram ads.

Make sure you are well aware of what will be going into making the ads to be able to come up with an effective budget for it.

Instagram Analytics

Analytics play a very important role when it comes to understanding the effectiveness of the content that is being sent out. It helps the company understand the reach and the engagement. It is therefore important to understand the different performance indicators that can help companies know the effectiveness of their ad campaigns being carried out on Instagram.

Reach

Reach refers to the number of people who can view the content that has been posted on the brand's page. This content has to be relevant and great for it to be popular on the platform's search tab in order to reach a bigger audience. If you go by benchmarks, then it will be easy to improve the content that is being sent out. It helps to build content that appeal to the audience and increases brand value. If the profile has a lot of views, it will be easy to draw in more people to follow the page and increase the product's reach.

Engagement

Customer engagement is an important part of using Instagram as a means to connect with the audience. It can be measured through the 'likes' and comments that have been posted for a picture. The comments usually include the brand's hashtag, which will help to understand the activity taking place. It is possible to track down a lot of information, such as the filters that are popular, the content that is selling best, and styles that are a hit etc. It will be best to carry out a trial and error to understand what is working well for your audience and use it as a benchmark to improve the content that is being put out on your page.

Here is a summary of what analytics can do for you:

- Reach out to more customers and keep them engaged.
- Measure the key performance indicators.
- Create a benchmark for customers.
- Collect and understand the data.

- Make changes and improvements in the posts with the data that is connected.

Chapter 10 YouTube Marketing

Live Streaming on YouTube

Like Facebook, YouTube offers live streaming functions. This allows you to display things in real time to anyone around the world. It offers a fun layout where you can highlight anything unique or of value to you.

Over the years YouTube has been used to stream various events live. It has streamed concerts, governmental meetings, conferences, sporting events, and much more. The audiences for these events can be impressive as well. For instance, in 2012 nearly eight million people went on YouTube to watch Felix Baumgartner jump out of an aircraft more than 20 miles above the earth's surface.

Fortunately, you don't have to be like Baumgartner and jump from the edge of the planet's atmosphere just to be noticed on YouTube. You just have to produce a smart video conference or other event to interact with people and share anything you want with them.

Live streaming works best when you want to talk with potential customers or wish to go to some special event, and share it online. Several steps must be used when getting a live stream ready.

Use the Stream Now Option

You can start streaming live by using the Stream Now option on your YouTube account. This works when you have an appropriate encoder. The Stream Now selector lets you get onto a streaming session on YouTube right away. Use this to send content at any time; YouTube will automatically start a stream when you get ready and end it when you finish.

1. Go to the Creator Studio and then the Live Streaming section.
2. *Set up your encoder.*

An encoder is a device or software program that compresses your audio and video into a setup that YouTube can support. You can download one of various encoders for your use including Webcam, Mobile Live, Air-Server, Sling-Studio, and Gameshow, among many others.

3. Enter a title and description for the video.
4. Add a thumbnail to your stream. This will let people know what your stream is about.
5. *Prepare a schedule for when the stream begins. It is recommended to let people know when you will stream ahead of time.*
6. Set your privacy setting.

You can make your live stream public or unlisted. Or a private session only available to subscribers, or people who enter with a password. If you wish to make it private, you will be prompted to enter a password for access or to use an option to let subscribers in.

7. Choose the latency option. High-quality latency is the best viewing quality; low-quality latency is best for real-time use.

8. If you only have the rights to the live content, click on the box to archive your stream as unlisted when finished.

Using the Events Option

You can also stream on YouTube through the Events option. The Events choice lets you plan your YouTube stream as a special occasion ahead of time.

1. Go to the Live Streaming section of the Creator Studio.

2. *Click the Events section and then the New Live Event option.*

3. Enter the basic points of the event.

The critical features to list include the title and description of the event, when it starts and ends, plus any tags you want to incorporate.

4. Set the privacy option. Use Public for events that appear on your channel.

5. *Select the Quick option. This will get the event supported through YouTube Live, the official live streaming support system used by YouTube.*

6. Make sure the item you use for recording yourself is accessible during the event.

Using Live Chat

The Live Chat feature on YouTube lets you interact with others during a live streaming event. This lets you talk to people online about anything happening in your stream.

The chat box appears on the right-hand side of your video player. It is visible when the video recording process is running.

How to use Live Chat:

1. Use either the Top chat or Live chat display. The Top chat option filters out possible spam messages. The Live chat displays everything.

2. *Assign a moderator for your chat. Click on the three dots near your chat box and enter someone's username to be approved as a moderator.*

Make sure the moderator is also someone within your business. The moderator will review all the things being entered into a live chat. The person should let you know what people are saying.

> 3. Go to the Community Settings section of the live chat and enter blocked words. Any chat messages that feature certain words will be blocked.

> 4. Block viewers from your live chat if they become abusive by clicking next to a questionable chat message, going to the writer's YouTube channel, and then clicking on the Block flag from the user's About page.

All the comments left during your chat will be accessible under your live streaming player after the stream ends.

Using Live Metrics

Make sure you read the live analytics or metrics on your streaming video. This gives you information on how many people are watching, how many messages are coming into your video, and how long people have been viewing your video and some other points.

You will not have access to every metric while you are recording. Use the YouTube Analytics feature to identify how your videos are working a few days after the stream ends.

Tips for Live Streaming

There are a few important tips when getting your live streaming experience on YouTube to work for you:

- Let people on YouTube know about your live stream as soon as possible. Tell them when you will stream so they can plan to get onto your page at a certain time.

- Keep a recorded archive of your live event on your hard drive if possible. This ensures you can get the event uploaded onto your page later on.

- Keep the stream looking professional. Use a high-quality camera and microphone to make your stream look its finest. Try to keep the microphone from being visible on the camera; a camera with a built-in microphone might be best.

- You have the option to use a webcam for streaming if needed. A webcam can work to get something ready for recording without having to use an encoder. Make sure the webcam is compatible with YouTube and that It's of good quality.

- Respond to comments during your live stream if possible. Address those who comment by name so people will see that you listen to them and that you have a vested interested in what they say.

- You can always record a live stream while on the go. Make sure the camera and microphone are steady so people can hear and see you properly.

A live stream on YouTube is fun because it offers a unique way to interact with people. Try this option to make your business visible on YouTube. Plan, so you have the best possible event ready.

Using Paid Ads on YouTube Through Google AdWords

The next point for using YouTube for your social media marketing is to utilize the paid ads feature on the site. The TrueView ad system lets you reach people who want to watch your videos on YouTube. Much of this is thanks to how YouTube works with the Google AdWords system.

Google AdWords is a method that lets people get their advertisements to appear higher up on a search. When a person's link is connected to a specific keyword, that link will appear at the top of a search page for that word. Since Google controls YouTube, it should not be difficult to use the marketing system offered here.

For YouTube, AdWords works a little differently. You will spend money on each click someone puts onto your video or every time someone watches your video. The videos and ads you produce will be displayed based on the keywords someone uses to search or the audience you target. The amount you spend depends on how many people click on your ad. A budget can also be set up so that your ad will be removed after you have spent a specified amount.

How Will Your Ad Be Displayed?

There are three ways your ad can be displayed on YouTube through AdWords:

1. It appears as a video that shows up before the desired video.

You can get your ad to play before someone's expected video comes up on YouTube. The user has the option to skip the ad after the first five seconds. You will only have to pay for the video ad when someone watches at least 30 seconds of it. An ad promoting the video will also appear on the top-right corner of the screen after the user watches or skips the video. The skip option makes it all the more important for you to draw the viewer's attention during the first few seconds of the ad.

2. *It could also show up on another website.*

Your video might appear on an outside website through an embedded player. Provided the video is similar in focus to the content on that site. You will pay for the ad when someone watches enough of the video.

3. It can appear on a YouTube search.

As with AdWords on Google, AdWords on YouTube will have your video appear at the top of a search listing. This is when the keyword someone searches for matches up with yours. You will pay money when someone clicks on the link.

Steps to Follow

1. Set up a Google AdWords account at adwords.google.com.

You will have to enter your contact information while also offer details on how you will pay for your ads.

2. *Go to the Campaigns tab and then click on the +Campaign option.*

3. Select the ad you want to work with. Enter the title of your ad, and the proper one should be displayed.

4. Enter the headline you wish to use.

5. *Write a few lines describing the ad.*

6. Determine where the ad will send people.

You can get the ad to redirect people to either your YouTube channel or your home page.

7. Choose the thumbnail you wish to display.

8. Determine the total amount of money you will spend on the ad. This includes how much you will spend for each click and the maximum budget.

The campaign will continue as long as it needs to. You can always remove your ad from the AdWords system on your own later if needed. Don't forget to include a proper payment system for how you will pay for the ads.

You can use a daily budget followed by the maximum cost-per-view. For instance, you could spend up to $0.05 per view for a $10 daily budget. This means your video can appear all day long until 200 people click or watch it and give you qualifying views. The total will reset the next day.

9. *Determine the audience that your video will target.*

Your target audience could be based on:

- Geographic location
- Age
- Gender
- Keyword interests

Make sure you enter the proper parameters based on the video you are promoting. Be specific if you have a particular need for marketing. Remember, your possible reach will shrink when you are more specific. The cost per click or view might also change depending on where you go.

Key Tips

- Always use proper keywords in your video's description.
- Keep the title appealing and friendly so that the user will want to see the ad.

- The content of your video should be relevant to whatever keywords you are incorporating into it.

- Get the viewer's attention as soon as possible. Get it in the first five seconds so the viewer will not skip your ad.

- Be free to tell a longer story if desired. Your video ad can last a few minutes if you want it to.

- Give viewers information on how to act at the end. Ask them to click on a link to your site or to subscribe to your channel.

- Use an end screen during the final ten seconds. The screen should tell the viewer what action to take.

- Be specific when entering in the demographics for your ad. Think about who might be interested in your business when getting this data entered.

What About Bumper Ads?

You can use bumper ads on YouTube if you prefer as well. A bumper ad is a six-second message that lets you create some buzz over what you have. It is not an ad that people can skip either; then again, it is a short commercial. You would have to create a new short ad that can be utilized as a bumper to make this option work.

1. Go to the Campaigns tab of your AdWords account and select the video you want to use. Make sure the ad is short enough to be a bumper.

2. *Go to the Video Ad Formats section and select the Bumper option.*

3. Prepare your budget.

4. Choose where you want to market your ads at.

5. *Save your advertisement.*

Prepare a unique and convenient six-second ad to make your bumper spot attractive and visible. It should be designed with a look that is interesting and special in some way. After all, you only have a limited amount of time to make it attractive.

Creating Ad Groups

Ad groups let you link several video advertisements together. The ads can work with the same budget and target the same people. You can get one ad group to target a specific audience while a second group focuses on a different grouping.

The steps for getting ad groups ready are as follows:

1. Go to the Campaigns section and click on the Ad Groups tab.

2. *Enter a name for the ad group.*

3. Enter the specific videos you want to use in the ad group.

4. Choose whether the ads will be ones listed on YouTube searches or in-stream ads that play before videos. You can only use one ad format at a time.

5. Enter the bid amount and budgeting information you wish to use plus the targeting options.

6. Save the ad group.

Your ad groups can be diverse and organized in many forms. You can produce one ad group that introduces people to your business. Another could feature videos that are for people who are already familiar with your brand. Keeping separate groups ready ensures you will establish ads that target different groups of people. You need to use different campaigns with multiple ad groups that work for everyone- ones who know who you are, those who want to know more, and the people who have no idea who you are.

Promote Your Channel

You may be thinking that this entire book is mostly about promoting your channel, and you'd be right, but promoting is actually an option on YouTube where you can spend money as well. YouTube gives everyone the option to "promote" their channel on the site. This means that you actually pay YouTube a sum of money and one or multiple of your videos will show up in special places on the website. If you've ever clicked on a video and an "ad" played beforehand, and it was more like a separate video than an ad, this was a promoted video. Promoting gives you the opportunity to have your video played before other people's videos of a related content, or shows up more commonly on recommended videos lists. It may put your video in the related videos section of other videos that aren't yours as well. Obviously, this is a really good option for spreading your channel around and gaining subscribers. There's not an easier way to promote your channel than this option. The question ultimately becomes whether the number of subscribers you gain is worth the amount of money you have to spend getting YouTube to promote your work. You have to have funds to pay for this promotion and this means having enough money budgeted in your company's marketing funds or having enough in your personal banking account to do so. If you believe the amount of fans you gain is worth the price, then it may be the best way to go.

If your YouTube channel is meant to promote your business to begin with, this is definitely a good option. Even if the promotion doesn't add that many followers to your YouTube channel, it still may add new customers to your business. This may be cheaper than running more conventional advertisement campaigns on television or other platforms. As mentioned earlier, the demographics that watch YouTube regularly are considerably younger, making advertising there a great way to attract a young and more hip customer base.

Just make sure that the content of your videos is not too controversial or inappropriate, as especially lately, YouTube has not been so keen on spreading these types of videos around their website, as it affects their advertisement options with other companies. If you have controversial content, it is still possible to promote, but it is recommended to use your least brazen videos to use this feature.

Chapter 11 Snapchat Marketing

Why use Snapchat?

This messaging app has come a long way, and it is estimated that it receives about 10 billion views a day and that the average user visits their Snapchat up to 18 times a day. So, what are the benefits of using Snapchat as a marketing tool?

1. No pressure

Unlike the early days of Facebook where most people worried about updating their statuses, Snapchat is relatively easy going. You can put as little or as much content as you want to and there's no pressure in that. Many businesses are too slow in acclimatizing themselves into Snapchat marketing, which has contributed to the laidback attitude toward the app. However, as video is set to become the biggest conduit of content, overtaking text, marketers will finally awaken to the utility of apps such as Snapchat. This app attracts more than three times YouTube's views. Even though marketers haven't totally warmed up to it, there are a ton of early birds who are minting money by marketing through the app.

2. Gain exposure

This app boasts an extremely active audience. Comprised mostly of young people, the average user checks their profile about 18 times a day. This means the engagement level is quite solid. If you'd craft a marketing message that users can identify with, you'd obviously gain a lot of engagement. Snapchat has also made it easy for people on other platforms to follow you. Once you create your account, you may update your other social media accounts with its QR code to let other people follow you. Unlike other platforms that seem to be hitting a plateau, Snapchat is on the rise and is set to break records in the near future.

3. Real-Time Marketing

Snapchat utilizes powerful structures and technology. One of the features is known as stories, where users get to watch time-limited videos. The latest feature allows users to send a screenshot of their watching stories to their friends. Marketers can take advantage of this feature by announcing discounts to whomever that watches the stories and brings out proof of the same at the store. As a video content site, Snapchat is at the forefront of ushering a new era, where video content trumps any other type of content. You can create engaging videos and upload them on your Snapchat and then offer incentives in order to garner the views.

4. Target locations

Snapchat allows marketers to interact with their followers not just on a real-time basis but also basing on location. Marketers can take advantage of this feature to promote their businesses and welcome their customers into intimate spaces of their lives. A marketing strategy that has a personal touch is always far more effective than cold words floating through the vast internet. When you have real-time communication with your followers, it becomes much easier to inspire them, educate them, and even bring out their tears. And as we know, emotion is the best prelude to conversion.

5. Build a community

Snapchat gives you the capability to form a community of believers around your brand. Such kind of thinking is what got Apple Inc to where it is today. Through Snapchat, you can establish a real-time connection with your followers, and get them to see what your brand is all about. Don't be quick to hard sell them as you may lose your genuineness. It's far much better to have the backing of a community as opposed to one person because they can spread the word around about your brand and products. A community inspires you even to create a better brand and feature-rich products. As they say, "Two hands are better than one," which is to say, your community can really chip in with ideas and suggestions. Your customers are goldmines of ideas. If you just give them a platform and a chance to speak frankly, they would open you up to many possibilities that you never once imagined. As a marketer, you must begin by accepting that you don't have all the answers and that when you hear of a good idea from some other person, you will have the courage to qualify that idea, and not trash it out of envy.

6. Less competition

For the majority of businesses, they are focused on sourcing leads from Twitter, Facebook, and Instagram. Most of them haven't caught up to the new wave of excitement around Snapchat. The earlier you start marketing your brand on Snapchat, the better for you. You will gain much more insight and practical tips, and by the time most businesses discover the magic of Snapchat, you will be some sort of Snapchat marketing legend, optimizing your campaigns in such a fashion that you spend least amounts of money to gain the most profit. With less competition, you have the perfect opportunity to test out various marketing styles and understand what really works for you.

7. High fun element

With most social media networks, the interaction is pretty basic and limited to text. But Snapchat creates an environment of fun by letting users share photos and videos in real time. With more fun, people loosen up, and the conversations become natural. This app enables marketers to free up their time without necessarily forgetting about their business. For instance, if you go away on holiday, you can keep posting random clips on Snapchat just to engage your followers. This is no time to hard sell, but rather a time to enjoy a pleasant moment with your followers.

8. Let your personality shine

Some people are too charismatic and have fun personalities. If you are such, then Snapchat is a great tool for boosting your conversions. Research shows that we tend to buy from people whom we like and trust. With a fun personality, people would no doubt be drawn to you, and it would boost their engagement with your brand, which would culminate into increased sales and brand visibility.

9. The value of trends

Use Snapchat to get your audience hooked on trending matters. If you want to be looked upon as a thought leader in your industry, you must be aware of all the trends and possess a deep and unique insight. You must have social currency. And when you attain the image of a thought leader, you earn people's trust, which eventually leads to a high conversion rate.

Snapchat symbols

This symbol appears next to a friend's name when you have both sent each other the most snaps.

💕 This symbol indicates a very tight friendship.

😬 The grimace shows you and another person are sharing a close friend.

🔥 When you have been exchanging snaps with another person for days on end.

⌛ When this symbol appears next to a friend's name, it means your Snap-streak is coming to an end.

🎂 This emoji shows up when your friend is celebrating their birthday.

Organic Snap-chat marketing

If you don't want to spend money, or don't have any money to spend, you can always expand your follower base organically and rely on them for revenue. Snapchat may be populated with extremely young people at present, but it is definitely poised to take over as video content becomes the dominant form of content consumption. It is in your best interests to get started promoting your brand on Snapchat.

Tell good stories

We are in 2019, but still, the tenets of a good story remain the same as far back in prehistory era. In order to attract a bigger fan base, you have to post exciting stories on your Snapchat. The following tips should help you tell good stories:

- Keep their eyes moving: as you go on with whatever you are saying or recording, try to shift your followers' angles and make them look around, it adds to the experience.

- Play with the features: Snapchat is an incredibly feature-rich app, just go ahead and play with those features and see how it goes. Use emojis, 3D stickers, filters, and geo-filters.

- Be concise: don't take a whole one-minute standing in the same boring position and saying a lot of nothing and expect to excite your followers. Brevity is the soul of wit. Be brief, but not so brief that meaning is lost.

Collaborate with others

You stand to gain a lot by collaborating with other industry players. Approach someone with a higher following on Snapchat and suggest that you do something together. This should be like a habit of yours. The more you collaborate with other people, the more cross-promotion will take place, and you will finally go viral.

Be responsive

Don't let the few thousand followers you have balloon your ego. If your loyal fans are sending you Snaps saying how cool they think you are, reply back and even give them a shout out. Your fans are always watching how you treat them.

Be consistent

It doesn't matter how great your first twenty stories were if you stopped doing it, if you stopped doing it consistently, you would slowly fall through the cracks into no man's land. You don't want that to happen. There will be bad days, of course. But have the courage to face those bad days so that you can have a reason to celebrate the good days.

Paid Snapchat marketing

Snapchat ads are tailored to help business owners reach their marketing goals by interacting with a young and super engaging audience. The advertisements are displayed between friends' stories and the content curated by Snapchat. If a Snapchatter is interested in an ad, they can swipe up in order to fulfill the call to action, which might be watching a longer video, reading an article or installing an app.

Pixel

It's basically an application embedded in your site that collects data about visitors' actions and behaviors.

Geo-filters

This tool helps advertisers target audiences in specific locations.

Lenses

Lenses are extremely popular among Snap-chatters as they integrate augmented reality. They use facial recognition technology to transform images.

Context Cards

Aimed at enticing users to click on the links, context cards add more info about a company into the ads.

Deep Links

These are links within an app that link out to other apps.

Snapchat Discover Ads

These ads cost $50000 per day and are obviously reserved for the high-budget companies. Your content is placed at the top of user Discover pages.

Common errors to avoid

Just as it is with other social media networks, there are considerable pitfalls you are at risk of falling into while marketing on Snapchat. These are some of the errors that you should be aware of and desist from:

1. Your stories are too long

If you post long stories, people might be discouraged from clicking. There's nothing wrong with taking your time to say whatever you want to. But then you should use a platform such as YouTube as it is suited for such kind of content. Snapchat users might be extremely active on the platform, but also they are restless. People don't want to have to watch an especially long story as it keeps them back from watching other Snaps that they consider fun. Perhaps the only time it's acceptable to post long stories is when you are making major announcements, not when you are promoting something.

2. Your stories are too short

If it is not okay to post long stories, would short stories do the trick? NO. If your story is so short that you don't communicate anything, then it is worse than even a long story. Always ensure that you provide sufficient context in order for the message to be passed across. Make sure that you are posting enough snaps that your story has a clear narrative and yet concise, and to make your story memorable and worthy use text, emojis and narration. The secret of a good story comes down to combining the features, letting your charisma shine, and ensuring that it is just the right length.

3. Posting Too Frequently

Another mistake that users might make is posting too frequently, forcing your followers to put up with your content. Less is more. Have some breaks to it. But if you are an ever-present fixture, you will slowly and irreversibly lose your shine, and finally, everyone will get tired of you and tell you as much. On Twitter, you might get away with shooting a new post every two hours, but on Snapchat it would be an incredibly bad idea. Focus on creating quality stories and uploading between evenly spaced out intervals. As a marketer, you may upload stories even twice or thrice in a week.

4. Failing to include a call to action

A call to action is an invitation for the user to perform some specific action. If you create a perfect story about the benefits of your new product and fail to ask your followers to click on the link, you have omitted a call to action. It might seem simple, but it is incredibly effective. As a marketer, you are a figure of authority, and you are supposed to guide your babies (followers) into taking the appropriate actions. Of course, some followers will figure out that they need to click on the call to action button, but then there are others who couldn't care less.

5. *You're too boring and predictable*

If you recycle a joke two times we will forgive you, but not a third time! The problem is not many people have taken the time to develop their personalities and become charismatic — also, not many people like researching before sitting down to come up with content. You will find that the average Snapchat user just starts talking into their phone without planning anything at all. That's the reason why it's hard to come across a consistently fun person to watch. Everyone appears to sound funny at the start, but then their well of ideas runs out, and they don't get out of their comfort zone, so they start to recycle old content, faintly at first, and then full blown with no trace of embarrassment. As a marketer, you must only post stories when you have something of value. Don't do it for the sake.

6. Having no sense of direction

You will hardly achieve anything without a clear direction. If today you are talking about women's clothes, and tomorrow you are talking about alternative medicine, and the day after tomorrow about ghosts, it shows that you have no clear direction. People won't take you seriously. Post content that is strictly tied to your brand. Of course, you can introduce fun aspects, narrations, and all other sweet little things, but ultimately you must steer your account with congruency. This is what will make you stand out and attract the audience that you have been seeking.

7. Not promoting your account

If your strategy is to post awesome content consistently with the hopes of going viral, that strategy might take forever. But to jumpstart your followers, you may need to promote your account. Start by telling your friends to follow you on Snapchat. And then get into sponsored content.

- Create a snap ad: this is a half-minute video that will appear alongside relevant content, and it will help you gain more followers.
- Choose sponsored geo-filters
- Offer interactive content

8. Posting at the wrong time

A snap appears for a few seconds before snuffing out and disappearing into the big jungle that is the internet. Knowing this, you must post stories at the appropriate times. This is when your target audience is most active.

9. Not using the localization feature

The localization feature is very critical. Users can leverage this feature to draw in people who are within the same area. This feature can help people take the conversation from the internet into a physical one. Sadly, a lot of people underutilize this feature, or not use it at all.

Chapter 12 LinkedIn

LinkedIn can be a profitable hotspot for web-based systems administration publicizing. It is definitely not hard to use and free, with in excess of 468 million people.

This is the place people plan to sort out, become progressively familiar with different associations, and develop their own one of a kind business circles. Despite what organization or thing a LinkedIn page addresses, it puts an individual, yet capable face on any association.

Coming up next are the best different ways LinkedIn can be used to grab attention from this group, and produce quality leads for your business.

Solicitation Recommendations

As the business person, when an individual profile has been set up and a couple of partners and delegates have been developed in the framework, it's basic to make a couple of request from these relation-ship for proposals. Solicitation that satisfied customers set up a few kind words, or solicitation that a careful agent do similarly. Repeat these exercises as habitually as could be normal considering the present situation, with the true objective to get the best reviews for your business and for your master works out. This is a basic bit of the collaboration that is significant on LinkedIn – people look for analysis on their things and organizations – get input (especially if it's certain).

React with Recommendations

Since internet organizing is set up in the relationship between people, it's furthermore comparably as basic to give out reviews and recommendations to accomplices and to clients. Be liberal and veritable. If a proposition is sincere, it will show up. Display how invigorating laborers are, and endorse appropriately. Afresh, this is a bit of the association that is basic in web based systems administration exhibiting with the ultimate objective to create leads dependent on trust and proclivity.

Make a Brand Group

An individual framework is unimaginable, and is basic on LinkedIn for showing the validity of the association, yet it won't reach past that orchestrate. Rather than spamming and sending requests self-assertively, which is significantly incapable (and too many spam standards can get a record confined on LinkedIn, fortuitously) for quality lead age; make a brand assembling and keep the option checked to "demonstrate this get-together in the Groups Directory" with the true objective to accomplish a much progressively broad framework.

Remember, LinkedIn has in excess of 468 million people. There are various people who may be enthusiastic about joining bundles for any number of topics; everything from SEO advancing, to exploratory composition. Thusly, make a social occasion that joins drawing in catchphrases in the title, or an average depiction to tell people what kind of get-together it is. At the point when the social event is completely operational, keep it invigorated with relevant focuses and mull over open trade. Partake, continually recollecting that the correspondence is the indispensable part to online life displaying.

Use Regular Profile Updates

Normal and relentless updates of a profile will keep it in the news channel, and can get eagerness from affiliations. Clearly, one wouldn't care to make profile revives that are pointless – that will simply serve to trouble relationship in case they have to consistently watch it in their news sources. In this manner, guarantee that they are proper updates, and take care of self-evident expertise.

Use an Image to Create an Image

It's a keen idea to have whatever number individual contacts as could sensibly be normal on both the LinkedIn profile page, and furthermore in the brand's social occasion page. Remember the 5 P's – exchange an exquisite, capable individual profile picture – it incorporates a human touch and urges relationship with interface and be destroyed in to one's profile. The other spot an image is fundamental is on the brand's social occasion page. Use the association's logo and put the business' best foot forward.

As an issue of first significance, online life displaying, paying little mind to what site, is about the joint effort among association and leads – between people – so exploit it by interfacing! A specialist atmosphere is continually basic, anyway significantly more so for the LinkedIn culture. Contact current customers, get endorsed to their allies, and tap into the more critical market through a brand gathering. This is an unprecedented technique to start on LinkedIn – it's straightforward and conceivable, and takes a base proportion of time concerning the publicist.

Chapter 13 Social Media Marketing Mistakes to Avoid

When you get on social media, it is important that you understand that your success is not guaranteed just because you created an account and shared a few posts. When it comes to social media, many businesses are trying to reach the same audience as you are, so you need to make sure that you stand out in the crowd. The market is far from being "tapped out," but if you come onto a platform without knowing how to use it effectively, you are quickly going to get overlooked as your audience favors brands who come in with a strategy.

In this chapter, you are going to learn what risks to avoid when using social media in general to ensure that you are not wasting your time using the wrong growth strategies online. You will learn what mistakes to avoid on each specific platform later, but for now, it is important that you understand the general risks to avoid so that you can have a massive impact online from day one.

Overstretching Yourself
Every single social media platform comes with a learning curve that you will need to endure in order to discover to master the platform and begin earning a high return on your social media marketing efforts. Regardless of whether or not you have already been on the platform, if you are not yet used to using that platform for marketing, you will need to learn

how to adjust your approach and ensure that it is optimized for marketing so that you can increase your earnings. When you are looking to use social media for marketing, it is important that you do not overstretch yourself as this can lead to not having the required attention to endure each learning curve and actually put that platform to use.

In order to ensure that you are not overstretching yourself, start by being honest about how much time you have each day to master your social media. If you only have a small amount of time per day or a few hours per week, it may be ideal to start out on the platform that is most likely to earn you an income. Then grow from there so that you are giving yourself enough time to thoroughly understand each platform. Once you have understood that first platform, then you can go ahead and start branching out to others so that you can master those as well.

Although you may want to grow big online quickly, it is important to understand where the balance lies when it comes to your growth. That is, it is a lot more productive to go big on one platform at a time, than it is to spread yourself so thin that none of your platforms gain traction and you miss the mark on every social media site you try. You will find that you master each platform and grow a lot more quickly this way, making it easier for you to start generating great success online relatively quickly.

Spending Time on the Wrong Platforms

Another big risk that you might make online is spending time on the wrong platforms or targeting the wrong parts of the platforms. If you are not directing your time and attention properly, you can quickly get drawn into taking actions that are not productive to your overall goal, which leaves you at risk of wasting a lot of time and not getting a lot of results.

Just because you may personally prefer one platform over another, or you may personally feel like one is better suited to your business compared to another, does not mean that this is actually the best choice. You need to go where your audience is and position yourself directly in front of them, or you are going to find yourself falling flat on your face online.

This way, you can ensure that you are focusing entirely on areas that will support you, rather than areas that will not.

Not Embracing the Learning Curve

When people get on social media, one of the biggest disservices they can do for themselves and their business is to fail to embrace the learning curve that comes with being on social media for marketing purposes. If you get on social media and fail to embrace the learning curve or try to do everything your way, you are going to find rather quickly that this is ineffective and that you are going to struggle to succeed online. While you certainly do need to embrace authenticity and freedom of expression online, failing to understand the basic concepts of how to get seen and heard online will only result in you struggling to grow your business.

The learning curve can take a few days, a few weeks, or even a few months depending on how much time you have to invest in social media and what you are doing to learn about the learning curve itself. If you want to accelerate this time, reading books like this one and paying attention to regular algorithm changes, new releases, and platform updates is a great opportunity to make sure that you are learning everything there is to know as quickly as possible. Aside from consuming the information, you also need to practice putting it to work online so that you can ensure that you are aware of both what the information is and how it works in practice. The more you read, learn, and integrate social media strategies online, the faster you will be at getting your business out there and for an online impact.

That being said, make sure that you are not going too quickly online, either. If you change your strategy too frequently, no matter what platform you are on, you will find yourself struggling to stay seen because people will grow confused with what it is that you are trying to achieve. You need to be willing to give each strategy the time required to allow it to accumulate reasonable results based on your efforts so that you can determine whether or not it worked, how it could have been improved, and what can be maintained when you start adjusting your strategies.

Blending Personal with Professional

Finally, even if you are running a personal brand, you need to be cautious about how much you blend your personal life with your professional life. Attempting to blend your personal and professional lives too much can result in you oversharing online and muddying the face of your business. You need to be cautious when it comes to building a brand, especially a personal one. You must ensure that you are not sharing information that could result in you taking away from the reputation or clarity of your business. In other words, even if you have a personal brand, keep your professional and personal lives separate to avoid having personal information leak into your business and destroy your professionalism.

Even if you are well-meaning, there will be many parts of your personal life that are simply not on-brand and, if you share them, it could result in you being seen as confusing or unprofessional. At the end of the day, even if you are sharing a personal brand, there are certain parts of your life that people simply do not want to read about or heed. The people who are following you will be more interested in the stuff that relates to them, or problems they may be facing, over anything else. This is not because people do not care about you, but because you are positioning yourself and your personal brand as a business. You need to be prepared to behave like a business.

If you do want to have a personal online platform, make sure that you keep your personal accounts private and separate from your business accounts. You can always share your business life with your personal friends but refrain from sharing your personal life with your business connections unless it in some way makes sense to your business. For example, if you are starting a fashion blog, you can share about fashion topics with your professional network but refrain from sharing about your love life or relationships unless it in some way can be tied into your outfit. If you were to wear a cute outfit on a date, for example, you could share this, but do not share about your hardships or troubles that your relationship may be facing online as this will only lead to you being seen as unprofessional. If you want to be seen as a professional business and have the opportunity to do business like a professional, you need to behave like a professional online at all times.

Conclusion

The next step is to begin researching other successful personal brands and why they interest you. Take the time to get an understanding of why they are successful. Then go on to complete the personal branding foundation checklist, realizing what you have to offer the world and how you can utilize what makes you unique and valuable to begin a long and fulfilling career. Continue to research possible mentors and idols, as well as new or innovative techniques and brands that you could admire and incorporate into your own efforts. Remember to take an honest and accurate gauge of the resources that are available to you, and use them with care and responsibility. When beginning to build your personal brand, remember to always be yourself and make an active and purposeful effort to curate a unique, styled, and marketable brand and image that will sell your persona and skills. No one else can be Martha Stewart, and no one else can be YOU.

www.ingramcontent.com/pod-product-compliance
Lightning Source LLC
Chambersburg PA
CBHW070639220526
45466CB00001B/231